£3·40.

Femmes  Women Hombres Men

Paul Verlaine

Femmes
Hombres

—

Women
Men

translated by
Alistair Elliot

Anvil Press Poetry

Published in hardback in 1979
by Anvil Press Poetry Ltd
69 King George Street London SE10 8PX
Reissued in paper covers 1982
Reprinted in 1983 (twice), 1987
ISBN 0 85646 086 9

Printed in Great Britain at
The Camelot Press Ltd, Southampton

This book is published
with financial assistance from
The Arts Council of Great Britain

for
KENNETH TYNAN
and
TONY HARRISON

Table

Contents

Introduction

IN JANUARY 1886 VERLAINE'S mother died. As a result of his handing over the last of her money for his separated wife, he himself became penniless, for the first time in his life, at the age of forty-one. He had no job, and the illness that had prevented him from attending his mother's funeral grew worse. After a six-week spell in hospital in the summer he wrote to a friend: 'I intend to go back to the arms of Public Assistance as soon as winter starts. Health and economy combined. I'll quarter myself for all the months in R in some Lariboisière or rather Hôtel-Dieu' (letter to Charles Morice, 30 October 1886).

Indeed, Verlaine did spend all but half of the next eight years in hospital. Remarks like the one just quoted, and the jocular tone of his accounts of hospital life, with their emphasis on the interest and aesthetic pleasure of living in these wonderful Paris buildings, might tempt the reader to conclude that he was simply exploiting the system. He tended to be popular with the hospital staff, and was allowed to have visitors during the day, and to work at night when the rest of the ward was asleep (most of the manuscript of *Hombres* is on Hôpital Broussais paper); and there, in the hospital bed, out of reach of the green goddess (absinthe), as Maurice Barrès put it, he regained his sense of direction and his inspiration. Certainly, it must have suited his temperament as well as his empty pocket, and one recalls his productivity in other protected circumstances: in prison (1873-4) and when school-teaching in Lincolnshire (1875). But he really was ill, and with a set of diseases that is not enviable at all: hydrarthrosis of the left knee (from 1885), exacerbated by rheumatism, ulcers due to an old but uncured bout of syphilis, diabetes, cirrhosis of the liver, cardiac hypertrophy (1886), complete anchylosis of the left knee, more syphilitic ulcers (1888), and infectious erysipelas of the left leg (1893); and finally, in January 1896, he died, aged fifty-one.

However, in *Femmes* and *Hombres* there is nothing of these realities (except the hint in the first line of 'Gamineries'), any more than of the life of a destitute man of letters in the streets outside. The world of the best poems here is made up of the happy minutes of people in bed, a continual *noce*—with the semi-religious felicity of a *wedding* superimposed on the sharp pleasures of *debauch*. Poem after poem contains only the parts of the body, not paid for, fed or clothed, just enjoyed and admired, even adored; and the people of the bodies are appreciated too.

It is almost entirely a humane and good-humoured book of sexual celebration, with the consequential sorrows (as Burns called them) completely passed over, and love never rearing its ugly head. The exception is that, as in the garden of Eden before the Fall, it is known that some things are less innocent than others, and this difficulty is occasionally alluded to and even (in the least successful poem of *Hombres*) argued against.

In the years when the poems in this book were being written (1888–91), whether he was in hospital or in cheap furnished rooms, Verlaine was, as always, working very hard. He published a great deal, with all the polishing and proof-reading that entails. Apart from poems and articles in magazines, his books of those years were:

1888: *Amour* (verse), in March
      Poètes maudits (prose), 2nd ed., in August
1889: *Parallèlement* (verse), in June
      Sagesse (verse), 2nd ed., in August
1890: *Dédicaces* (41 poems)—various months cited
      Femmes (verse), in December
1891: *Bonheur* (verse), at the end of April
      Choix de poésies, in June
      Mes hôpitaux (prose), in November
      Chansons pour elle (verse), in December

and finally, in April 1892, *Liturgies intimes* (verse) was published less than a month after the date by which all the poems of *Hombres* must have been completed.

Many of the poems in *Sagesse*, *Parallèlement* and *Amour* had been written long before they were published in these collections—some as much as sixteen years before—but a crude tabulation of just some of the poems Verlaine is known to have composed between 1887 and 1892 is as impressive as the list of his publications of those years:

Dédicaces (41 poems, mainly sonnets, in the first edition)—early
      1888–October 1889
Bonheur (33 poems)—early 1887–January 1891
Chansons pour elle (25 poems)—probably March–October 1891
Odes en son honneur (19 poems)—summer 1891–January 1892

There is something heroic about such activity under such conditions. But Verlaine was always productive, and indeed interested in his productivity: throughout his life he was apt to note, in letters to friends or on the manuscripts themselves, the number of verses he had just composed. Of some of this late verse someone unkindly remarked: 'la littérature la plus alimentaire'—it was one of Verlaine's editors, unselfconsciously biting the hand that fed him.

For the rest, Verlaine's life during these difficult years was not the calm idyll of this book. Although by 1890 he was beginning to make substantial amounts of money from his books and from lecture tours abroad and readings, he was so spendthrift with it, and his two awful but beloved mistresses so dishonest, that he remained a poverty-stricken writer of begging letters to the end. But it seems significant that the only two clearly identifiable people in these poems made only brief appearances in Verlaine's actual life, so for further details I simply refer the reader to Joanna Richardson's biography of the poet, or, better still, J. H. Bornecque's readable, indeed re-readable and profound little book *Verlaine par lui-même*, or, best of all, for insight and pleasure, to the volumes of Verlaine's 'unpublished correspondence' (as the French say) that have been edited and annotated by Georges Zayed.

II

The poems gathered together in this volume appeared originally as two separate books. *Femmes* was published by Kistemaeckers in Brussels at the end of 1890 (with the date 1891 on the title page, and the author's name given as 'Pablo de Herlagnez'—a pseudonym Verlaine had used before). *Hombres* was posthumous, appearing in Paris in 1904 or late 1903 (both dates are cited by bibliographers), being published by Messein, the successor to the business of Verlaine's publisher Léon Vanier.

'Published' is not quite the right word for the first appearance of these books, as they both came out *sous le manteau*, that is, clandestinely. In fact, there is still no good modern edition of them in print in France, and only six of the poems are in the Pléiade Verlaine, which is therefore not exactly truthful in calling itself the *Œuvres poétiques complètes*. Even the best edition of Verlaine's *Œuvres complètes*, edited by H. de Bouillane de Lacoste and Jacques Borel (Club du meilleur livre, 2 vols.,

1959–60), hesitated to include them and came out in two versions, so that only a quarter of the copies of that edition contain these *Œuvres libres*. That authoritative text, edited by Jacques Borel, is the one gratefully followed here, with ten exceptions which are detailed among the notes at the end of the book.

The poems in *Femmes* were written between 1888 and 1890, and Verlaine seems to have seen them, at least at first, as additions to the 'Filles' section of his book *Parallèlement* (1889). In fact, in a letter to Vanier (7 January 1892) he proposed adding some of them to the second edition of the book (1894), but this did not happen. The manuscript of *Femmes* still survives, but is in private hands, and was checked for the Club du meilleur livre edition by Georges Zayed. Oddly enough, it did not emerge at the time that there were two other relevant but un-published poems in the *Femmes* manuscript. These were later published by Professor Zayed in his edition of Verlaine's *Lettres inédites à Charles Morice* (1964), where it was also revealed that the owner of the manu-script was Jean Gimpel. I have included these two poems as an appendix.

Most of the poems in *Hombres* were written in 1891. The exceptions are 'Sur une statue' (written in Aix-les-Bains in 1889), 'Rendez-vous' (the first version, in five stanzas, was written in 1887) and two poems written in the *Album Zutique*, a kind of visitors' book kept by a group of literary friends and contributed to by Verlaine and Rimbaud in 1871 and 1872. These two are 'Dizain ingénu' (originally called 'Remem-brances' and lacking the present opening couplet) and 'Le sonnet du trou du cul', of which the sextet was composed by Rimbaud.

Verlaine's complete manuscript of *Hombres* was given away by him, in bits, but the Fonds Doucet (more formally, the Bibliothèque Littéraire Jacques Doucet) in Paris possesses a manuscript of the book in his writing, complete except for the last two poems in the book as we have it here: that is, except for the unfinished poem 'O mes amants . . .' and 'Le sonnet du trou du cul'. Both of these are, however, included in another Fonds Doucet manuscript, the copy of *Hombres* made by Vanier on 19 March 1892. Vanier wrote on his copy 'pendant du volume obscène *Femmes*', citing Verlaine's own expression about these poems (in the letter already mentioned), so it is probably right to see *Hombres*, short and presumably incomplete as it is, as part of a book, of which *Femmes* is no more than another, or the other, part.

My translations owe much to the circumstances in which I began work on them. The first eight to be done were commissioned by Kenneth Tynan for his show *Carte Blanche*: these were 'Ouverture', 'Partie carrée', 'Billet à Lily', 'Au bal', 'Reddition', 'Régals', 'Hommage dû' and 'Le sonnet du trou du cul'. When these versions were finished, it seemed natural to continue work on others for a complete parallel-text edition of *Femmes* and *Hombres* since both are out of print everywhere, except for Curt Moreck's attractive edition of *Femmes* with German translation, and a facsimile reprint of the 'first original clandestine edition' of *Amies, Femmes* and *Hombres*.

Finally, I must express my gratitude to Kenneth Tynan and Clifford Williams for encouraging me to publish the two poems ('Au bal' and 'Reddition') that were eventually used in *Carte Blanche*, in a more than somewhat different form.

I should also like to thank M. François Chapon of the Bibliothèque Littéraire Jacques Doucet for his help both with some textual cruces in *Hombres* and with a number of problems of interpretation or reference; and Professor Georges Zayed of Boston College, for agreeing with or correcting my views on certain textual cruces in *Femmes* and in the two poems he was the first to publish, and for his marvellous editions (already mentioned) of Verlaine's letters. My shyer English helpers will no doubt be content to be thanked anonymously.

All errors are my own.

ALISTAIR ELLIOT

Since this Introduction was written I have seen another edition of Verlaine's 'Œuvres libres' entitled, misleadingly, *Hombres*, edited by H. Juin and published in Paris in 1977 by Régine Deforges. It is closely based on the Club du meilleur livre edition, with similar textual notes (on punctuation and revisions) but without general annotations.

A.E.

Femmes

Women

Ouverture

Je veux m'abstraire vers vos cuisses et vos fesses,
Putains, du seul vrai Dieu seules prêtresses vraies,
Beautés mûres ou non, novices ou professes,
O ne vivre plus qu'en vos fentes et vos raies!

Vos pieds sont merveilleux, qui ne vont qu'à l'amant,
Ne reviennent qu'avec l'amant, n'ont de répit
Qu'au lit pendant l'amour, puis flattent gentiment
Ceux de l'amant qui las et soufflant se tapit,

Pressés, fleurés, baisés, léchés depuis les plantes
Jusqu'aux orteils, sucés les uns après les autres,
Jusqu'aux chevilles, jusqu'aux lacs des veines lentes,
Pieds plus beaux que des pieds de héros et d'apôtres!

J'aime fort votre bouche et ses jeux gracieux,
Ceux de la langue et des lèvres et ceux des dents
Mordillant notre langue et parfois même mieux,
Truc presque aussi gentil que de mettre dedans;

Et vos seins, double mont d'orgueil et de luxure,
Entre quels mon orgueil viril parfois se guinde
Pour s'y gonfler à l'aise et s'y frotter la hure:
Tel un sanglier és vaux du Parnasse et du Pinde.

Vos bras! j'adore aussi vos bras si beaux, si blancs,
Tendres et durs, dodus, nerveux quand faut, et beaux
Et blancs comme vos culs et presque aussi troublants,
Chauds dans l'amour, après, frais comme des tombeaux.

Openers

I want to get away into your thighs and cheeks,
You whores, the one true god's only true priestesses,
Whether you're long sworn in, green beauties or antiques:
O to live only in your clefts and cleavages.

Your marvellous feet, that only take you out to get
A lover, only bring you back for lovers, rest
Only in bed at lovetime till they smoothly pet
The lover's feet as he lies panting on the nest—

Your feet, so squeezed and sniffed and kissed and licked, from soles
To toes, each toe mouth-organed, and then ankles too,
With their slow veins that snake in coils toward their holes,
Lovelier than saints' or heroes' feet, and what they do.

And how I love your mouth: its games so full of grace
They make the lips begin to seek, the tongue to hide,
The teeth to nibble tongue, or something in its place—
Such tricks are almost better than it is inside.

And then your breasts, the double mount of pride and lust:
Between them my male pride sometimes goes chimneying
And swelling rubs there like a wild boar in the dust
On Mount Parnassus till its head begins to sing.

Your arms, so fine, so pale, excite my reverence:
Tender and hard, and sinewy at need, but plump
And warm in love, though after chilled as monuments,
So pale, so fine, they stir my senses like your rump.

Et les mains au bout de ces bras, que je les gobe!
La caresse et la paresse les ont bénies,
Rameneuses du gland transi qui se dérobe,
Branleuses aux sollicitudes infinies!

Mais quoi! Tout ce n'est rien, Putains, aux prix de vos
Culs et cons dont la vue et le goût et l'odeur
Et le toucher font des élus de vos dévots,
Tabernacles et Saints des Saints de l'impudeur.

C'est pourquoi, mes sœurs, vers vos cuisses et vos fesses
Je veux m'abstraire tout, seules compagnes vraies,
Beautés mûres ou non, novices ou professes,
Et ne vivre plus qu'en vos fentes et vos raies.

I   A celle que l'on dit froide

Tu n'es pas la plus amoureuse
De celles qui m'ont pris ma chair;
Tu n'es pas la plus savoureuse
De mes femmes de l'autre hiver.

Mais je t'adore tout de même!
D'ailleurs, ton corps doux et bénin
A tout, dans son calme suprême,
De si grassement féminin,

My admiration wanders down those arms to hands:
Hands that from lazing and caressing are so fair,
Hands that revive our numb and softly shrinking glands
And wag them with an infinitely worried care.

Well, all that beauty's nothing, whores, compared with your
Arses and cunts which give the feels of Paradise—
We know we'll go there by this haze of sensual awe—
Holies of Holies, Arks of Covenants of vice.

That's why I want to get into your thighs and cheeks,
My Sisters, far away, in the best mate there is,
Whether you're long sworn in, green beauties or antiques,
And so live only in your clefts and cleavages.

I   To the one they call cold

You are not the most fond of love
Of women who have tried me on;
You are not the most spicy of
My women of the year just gone,

But I adore you anyway!
Besides, your sweet, mild body in
Its final calm knows how to say
All that is fatly feminine,

De si voluptueux sans phrase,
Depuis les pieds longtemps baisés
Jusqu'à ces yeux clairs purs d'extase,
Mais que bien et mieux apaisés!

Depuis les jambes et les cuisses
Jeunettes sous la jeune peau,
A travers ton odeur d'éclisses,
Et d'écrevisses fraîches, beau,

Mignon discret, doux petit Chose
A peine ombré d'un or fluet,
T'ouvrant en une apothéose
A mon désir rauque et muet,

Jusqu'aux jolis tétins d'infante,
De miss à peine en puberté,
Jusqu'à ta gorge triomphante
Dans sa gracile vénusté,

Jusqu'à ces épaules luisantes,
Jusqu'à la bouche, jusqu'au front
Naïfs aux mines innocentes
Qu'au fond les faits démentiront,

Jusqu'aux cheveux courts bouclés comme
Les cheveux d'un joli garçon,
Mais dont le flot nous charme, en somme,
Parmi leur apprêt sans façon,

En passant par la lente échine
Dodue à plaisir, jusques au
Cul somptueux, blancheur divine,
Rondeurs dignes de ton ciseau,

In short, all that's voluptuous,
Right from your long-kissed feet to those
Clear eyes free of ecstatic fuss,
That pleasures only re-compose!

Up from the young skin that reveals
Yet younger shapes of legs and thighs,
Across the salty smells of creels
And crayfish newly caught that rise

From where your shy, small, dainty thing—
Veiled in gold hairs, but only just—
Like a mandorla opening
Gapes for my hoarse and speechless lust,

Up to that pretty-princess breast
Of barely nubile governess
And the real triumph of your chest,
The neck's inhuman loveliness,

Then to the shoulders' hint of gloss
And to the forehead, mouth and eye
Untouched by sexual gain and loss—
Until one sees the ways you lie—

Up to your hair, done short in curls
As pretty boys might let it grow,
But when the weight of it unfurls
More charming in its careless flow

Rippling down your long, slow spine
(So nice and plump), until it comes
To sumptuous whiteness quite divine:
A bum as round as Canova's bums

Mol Canova! jusques aux cuisses
Qu'il sied de saluer encor,
Jusqu'aux mollets, fermes délices,
Jusqu'aux talons de rose et d'or!—

Nos nœuds furent incoercibles?
Non, mais eurent leur attrait, leur.
Nos feux se trouvèrent terribles?
Non, mais donnèrent leur chaleur.

Quant au Point, Froide? non pas, Fraîche,
Je dis que notre «sérieux»
Fut surtout, et je m'en pourlèche,
Une masturbation mieux,

Bien qu'aussi bien les prévenances
Sussent te préparer sans plus—
Comme tu dis—d'inconvenances,
Pensionnaire qui me plus,

Et je te garde entre les femmes
Du regret, non sans quelque espoir,
De quand peut-être nous aimâmes
Et de sans doute nous r'avoir.

Septembre 1889

But softer to the tool, and thighs
To whom a standing *encore*'s due,
Calves, the strong jambs of paradise,
And lastly, pink-gold heels, to you!

So were love's knots unbreakable?
No, just a weak magnetic bond.
Our passion torrid? Tropical?
Well, no; but it was . . . warm, and . . . fond.

And, are you cold? No, I'd say: cool.
I'd say our most romantic boff—
I lick my lips and start to drool—
Was a superior tossing-off,

For me—though my attentions stirred
Your feelings too, but nothing more
Unsuitable (to use your word);
So, schoolgirl whom I still adore,

I keep you on my active list
Of women, full of hope, though sad,
About the love we made (or missed)
And second chances to be had.

2   Partie carrée

Chute des reins, chute du rêve enfantin d'être sage,
    Fesses, trône adoré de l'impudeur,
Fesses, dont la blancheur divinise encor la rondeur,
Triomphe de la chair mieux que celui par le visage!

Seins, double mont d'azur et de lait aux deux cimes brunes
    Commandant quel vallon, quel bois sacré!
Seins, dont les bouts charmants sont un fruit vivant, savouré
Par la langue et la bouche ivres de ces bonnes fortunes!

Fesses, et leur ravin mignard d'ombre rose un peu sombre
    Où rôde le désir devenu fou,
Chers oreillers, coussins au pli profond pour la face ou
Le sexe, et frais repos des mains après ces tours sans nombre!

Seins, fins régals aussi des mains qu'ils gorgent de délice,
    Seins lourds, puissants, un brin fiers et moqueurs,
Dandinés, balancés, et, se sentant forts et vainqueurs,
Vers nos prosternements comme regardant en coulisse!

Fesses, les grandes sœurs des seins vraiment, mais plus nature,
    Plus bonhomme, sourieuses aussi,
Mais sans malice trop et qui s'abstiennent du souci
De dominer, étant belles pour toute dictature!

Mais quoi! Vous quatre, bons tyrans, despotes doux et justes,
    Vous impériales et vous princiers,
Qui courbez le vulgaire et sacrez vos initiés,
Gloire et louange à vous, Seins très saints, Fesses très augustes!

Where the waist falls, where childhood's dream of being good
    Falls to the buttocks, throne of our disgrace,
Where fleshly beauty triumphs more than in the face,
Buttocks, where white and round form a Beatitude!

Breasts, double mount of blue and milk with two brown crests
    Commanding views of dale and sacred wood,
Breasts, whose delightful tips like living fruit are food
To tongue and mouth drunk on these coupled fortunes, breasts!

Buttocks, their delicate gully full of dark pink shade
    Where lust prowls madly down the downy trail,
Dear pillows, cushion deeply creased for nose or tail,
A cool place to rest hands when all their tricks are played!

Breasts, to the hands they fill a feast of delicate size,
    Breasts heavy, strong, proud and contemptuous,
Cradled and rocked, feeling they've won, looking at us
And our prostrations from the corners of their eyes!

Buttocks, big sisters of the breasts, more natural
    And open, parted in a candid smile,
So simple they don't care to bully or beguile,
All their dictatorship just being beautiful.

Here I invoke you four: tyrants, but sweet and just,
    The imperial pair, the princely underlings,
That bend the vulgar and admit anointed kings,
Hosannah, Rumpus Rex and Venerable Bust!

3   Triolets à une vertu
pour s'excuser du peu

A la grosseur du sentiment
Ne va pas mesurer ma force,
Je ne prétends aucunement
A la grosseur du sentiment.
Toi, serre le mien bontément
Entre ton arbre et ton écorce.
A la grosseur du sentiment
Ne va pas mesurer ma force.

La qualité vaut mieux, dit-on,
Que la quantité, fût-ce énorme.
Vive un gourmet, fi du glouton!
La qualité vaut mieux, dit-on.
Allons, sois gentille et que ton
Goût à mon désir se conforme.
La qualité vaut mieux, dit-on,
Que la quantité, fût-ce énorme.

Petit poisson deviendra grand
Pourvu que L'on lui prête vie.
Sois ce L'on-là; sur ce garant
Petit poisson deviendra grand,
Prête-*la* moi, je te *le* rend.—
Rai gaillard et digne d'envie.
Petit poisson deviendra grand
Pourvu que L'on lui prête vie.

Mon cas se rit de ton orgueil,
Etant fier et de grand courage.
Tu peux bien en faire ton deuil.

3   Triolets for a virtue
in excuse for mine being small

Great length and breadth in what you feel
Is different from how deep it goes.
I wouldn't claim for my appeal
Great length and breadth in what you feel.
Come kindly though, and clinch my deal
Where—between flesh and blood—it rose.
Great length and breadth in what you feel
Is different from how deep it goes.

For quality is best, they say,
However large the quantity.
The glutton yields to the gourmet,
For quality is best, they say.
Be nice: come, let your taste betray
To my desire that they agree.
For quality is best, they say,
However large the quantity.

Small fish get big as they can be
If Someone lends them Life enough.
Oh, be that Someone: guarantee
Small fish get big as big can be.
I'll pay you back what you lend me:
That joyful enviable stuff!
Small fish get big as big can be
If Someone lends them Life enough.

This point pokes fun at all your pride,
Standing up proud and stout of heart.
Give in: be on the yielding side.

Mon cas se rit de ton orgueil
Comme du chat qui n'a qu'un œil,
Et te voue au «dernier outrage».
Mon cas se rit de ton orgueil
Etant fier et de grand courage.

Tout de même et sans trop de temps
C'est fait. *Sat prata*. L'ordre règne.
Sabre au clair et tambours battants
Tout de même et sans trop de temps!
Bien que pourtant, bien que contents
Mon cas pleure et ton orgueil saigne.
Tout de même et sans trop de temps
C'est fait. *Sat prata*. L'ordre règne.

This point pokes fun at all your pride
As at that pussy that's one-eyed,
And dooms you to the outraged part.
This point pokes fun at all your pride,
Standing up proud and stout of heart.

Notwithstanding, the time soon comes:
It's done. Well watered. Order reigns.
With drawn sword and a tuck of drums,
Not with standing, the time soon comes.
Now joy and virtue do their sums:
My point weeps; pride bleeds; who complains?
Not withstanding, the time soon comes:
It's done. Well watered. Order reigns.

Louis Quinze aimait peu les parfums. Je l'imite
Et je leur acquiesce en la juste limite.
Ni flacons, s'il vous plaît, ni sachets en amour!
Mais, ô qu'un air naïf et piquant flotte autour
D'un corps, pourvu que l'art de m'exciter s'y trouve;
Et mon désir chérit, et ma science approuve
Dans la chair convoitée, à chaque nudité,
L'odeur de la vaillance et de la puberté
Ou le relent très bon des belles femmes mûres.
Même j'adore—tais, morale, tes murmures—
Comment dirais-je? ces fumets, qu'on tient secrets,
Du sexe et des entours, dès avant comme après
La divine accolade et pendant la caresse,
Quelle qu'elle puisse être, ou doive, ou le paraisse.
Puis, quand sur l'oreiller mon odorat lassé,
Comme les autres sens, du plaisir ressassé,
Somnole et que mes yeux meurent vers un visage
S'éteignant presque aussi, souvenir et présage
De l'entrelacement des jambes et des bras,
Des pieds doux se baisant dans la moiteur des draps,
De cette langueur mieux voluptueuse monte
Un goût d'humanité qui ne va pas sans honte,
Mais si bon, mais si bon qu'on croirait en manger!
Dès lors, voudrais-je encor du poison étranger,
D'une fragrance prise à la plante, à la bête,
Qui vous tourne le cœur et vous brûle la tête,
Puisque j'ai, pour magnifier la volupté,
Proprement la quintessence de la beauté!

Louis the Well-Loved didn't care for scent.
Nor I. I bear it, to a just extent,
But let a pungent waft of nature float
Around a body that excites this goat:
No little bottles, no sachets in love!
Experience and my fondest lust approve
In the desired flesh, at each nudity,
The odours of rude health and puberty
Or a good whiff of fine ripe womanhood.
I even relish—censor, down, be good!—
Those little fumes that genitals secrete
And we keep secret, till we kneel and meet
For holy accolades, those fumes we find
In the caress itself, whatever kind.
Then, when the pillow holds my sense of smell
Tired like the others, having felt so well,
And snoozing, when eyes dull and all but close
In someone's face, a happy sign that shows
Memories and hopes of twining limbs, when feet
Kiss gently down there under their damp sheet,
Then from that still more sensual faintness rise
Tastes of humanity that some despise,
A breath of shame, but good, so good you'd eat it.
After that, could I want a foreign, fetid
Venom from some plant's crotch, some beast's behind,
That makes your heart thump and burns out your mind?—
When magnifying pleasure every day
I've beauty in its essence: our bouquet!

5   Filles

I

Bonne simple fille des rues,
Combien te préféré-je aux grues

Qui nous encombrent le trottoir
De leur traîne, mon décrottoir,

Poseuses et bêtes poupées
Rien que de chiffons occupées

Ou de courses et de paris,
Fléaux déchaînés sur Paris!

Toi, tu m'es un vrai camarade
Qui la nuit monterait en grade

Et même dans les draps câlins
Garderait des airs masculins,

Amante à la bonne franquette,
L'amie à travers la coquette

Qu'il te faut bien être un petit
Pour agacer mon appétit.

Oui, tu possèdes des manières
Si farceusement garçonnières

Qu'on croit presque faire un péché
(Pardonné puisqu'il est caché),

5   Girls

I

Good simple street-girl, much preferred
To that more plumaged sort of bird

That crowds the pavement with its skirt
(On which I free my shoes of dirt):

Stupid as dolls they swank and pose,
Their heads quite empty but for clothes

And racing and the betting-odds—
Plagues loosed on Paris by the gods!

But you're a comrade, a real mate
(At night promoted up a state)

Who even where the sheets caress
Preserve your air of manliness,

Lover who frankly comes and gets,
And friend who if need be coquettes

A little, sometimes, to relight
My pilot-flame of appetite.

Or else you've ways so like a boy's
(Which one hilariously enjoys)

It almost seems this is that sin
One's pardoned if one's secret in,

Sinon que t'as les fesses blanches
De frais bras ronds et d'amples hanches

Et remplaces ce que n'as pas
Par tant d'orthodoxes appas.

T'es un copain tant t'es bonne âme.
Tant t'es toujours tout feu, tout flamme

S'il s'agit d'obliger les gens
Fût-ce avec tes pauvres argents

Jusqu'à doubler ta rude ouvrage,
Jusqu'à mettre du linge en gage!

Comme nous t'as eu des malheurs
Et tes larmes valent nos pleurs

Et tes pleurs mêlés à nos larmes
Ont leurs salaces et leurs charmes,

Et de cette pitié que tu
Nous portes sort une vertu.

T'es un frère qu'est une dame
Et qu'est pour le moment ma femme . . .

Bon! puis dormons jusqu'à potron-
Minette, en boule, et ron, ron, ron!

Serre-toi, que je m'acoquine
Le ventre au bas de ton échine,

Mes genoux emboîtant les tiens,
Tes pieds de gosse entre les miens.

36

But that your arse is white and bland,
Your cool arms round, your haunches grand—

And your perplexing lack of cock's
Made good by charms more orthodox.

Yes, you're a pal: kind soul, you burn
To do your neighbour a good turn

And to oblige one even use
Your meagre savings (all in sous),

Go out to work your rough hours twice
And hock your sheets, just to be nice.

Like us, you've had hard times, and when
You weep, you win our tears again,

And as the teardrops mix I feel
And taste your salty, strong appeal,

And from the pity you bestow
On us, good things begin to flow.

You're like a brother with a quim
That's wedded now to my fifth limb . . .

Ohh! now let's sleep till cocks can stir
And grow: let's curl up too, and purr.

Squeeze in as I relax and line
My belly up your lower spine,

My knees just locking over yours,
My feet outside your little paws,

Roule ton cul sous ta chemise,
Mais laisse ma main que j'ai mise

Au chaud sous ton gentil tapis.
Là! nous voilà cois, bien tapis.

Ce n'est pas la paix, c'est la trève.
Tu dors? Oui. Pas de mauvais rêve.

Et je somnole en gais frissons,
Le nez pâmé sur tes frisons.

II

Et toi, tu me chausses aussi,
Malgré ta manière un peu rude
Qui n'est pas celle d'une prude
Mais d'un virago réussi.

Oui, tu me bottes quoique tu
Gargarises dans ta voix d'homme
Toutes les gammes du rogomme,
Buveuse à coude rabattu!

Mais femme! sacré nom de Dieu!
A nous faire perdre la tête,
Nous foutre tout le reste en fête
Et, nom de Dieu, le sang en feu.

Ton corps dresse, sous le reps noir,
Sans qu'assurément tu nous triches,
Une paire de nénés riches,
Souples, durs, excitants, faut voir!

And roll your petticoat around
Your bum, but leave my hand—it's found

A warm spot under your sweet rug.
There we are, quiet, good, and snug.

Only a truce—it isn't peace.
You sleeping? Yes. No nightmares, please.

And shivering happily, my nose
Swooning upon your curls, I doze.

II

And you as well, you suit me too:
Although your manner's a bit grim,
It's not the harshness of the prim,
You great unexpurgated shrew.

Yes, we get on—despite the noise
You gargle out, right down the scale
Of whisky voices to the male,
Lifting your elbow with the boys!

All woman, though—my God!—for you
Turn off our common sense, and knock
Our other senses all to cock,
As if we'd only you to do.

Your body trims with gentle slaps
Under black rep a moving couple
Of tits so rich and hard and supple
We know they can't be booby-traps,

Et moule un ventre jusqu'au bas,
Entre deux friands hauts-de-cuisse,
Qui parle de sauce et d'épice
Pour quel poisson de quel repas?

Tes bas blancs—et je t'applaudis
De n'arlequiner point tes formes—
Nous font ouvrir des yeux énormes
Sur des mollets que rebondis!

Ton visage de brune où les
Traces de robustes fatigues
Marquent clairement que tu brigues
Surtout le choc des mieux râblés,

Ton regard ficelle et gobeur
Qui sait se mouiller puis qui mouille,
Où toute la godaille grouille
Sans reproche, ô non! mais sans peur,

Toute ta figure—des pieds
Cambrés vers toutes les étreintes
Aux traits crépis, aux mèches teintes,
Par nos longs baisers épiés—

Ravigote les roquentins,
Et les ci-devant jeunes hommes
Que voilà bientôt que nous sommes,
Nous électrise en vieux pantins,

Fait de nous de vrais bacheliers,
Empressés autour de ta croupe,
Humant la chair comme une soupe,
Prêts à râler sous tes souliers!

And moulds a belly to that keel,
Between two luscious inner thighs,
That speaks of bubbling sauce and spice—
But for what fish and at what meal?

And your white stockings—I applaud
That scorn of harlequin disguise—
Stagger us, making our round eyes
Bulge like your calves, they are so broad!

Brown woman's face—we read the tracks
Of heavy man-hours on your skin,
Clear signs that you go out to win
The hard grind of the strongest backs—

Those cunning, goofy eyes of yours,
Able to water and then come
Rolling with booze and looking rum,
Hardly a parfit gentil whore's,

And your whole figure, right from feet
Arched towards every known embrace
To your dyed locks and rough-cast face
Spied on while lips do more than meet,

All this revives us rakish wrecks
And former younger men that fate
Reforms so soon into 'the late',
Pours back the current through our flex,

And makes us old blocks feel so chipper
We fuss like students round your crupper,
Sniffing as if we'd come for supper
Or else to croak across your slipper!

Tu nous mets bientôt à quia,
Mais, patiente avec nos restes,
Les accommodes, mots et gestes,
En ragoûts où de tout y a.

Et puis, quoique mauvaise au fond,
Tu nous as de ces indulgences!
Toi, si teigne entre les engeances,
Tu fais tant que les choses vont.

Tu nous gobes (ou nous le dis)
Non de te satisfaire, ô goule!
Mais de nous tenir à la coule
D'au moins les trucs les plus gentils.

Ces devoirs nous les déchargeons,
Parce qu'au fond tu nous violes,
Quitte à te fiche de nos fioles
Avec de plus jeunes cochons.

You show us pretty soon what's what,
But patient with such remnants use
Our bits and pieces up in stews
Where everything goes in the pot.

And then, though really bad, you see
What we can do, and do us proud!
However bitchy with your crowd,
You make all this go swimmingly.

You go for us (or so you say)
Not for the blow-out—greedy-guts!
But so's to keep the poor old nuts
Up to the nicest tricks to play.

In fact, you rape us, really. Fine:
That means that we've discharged all debts
When you make fun of our pipettes
In bed with other, younger swine.

6   A Madame * * *

Quand tu m'enserres de tes cuisses
La tête ou les cuisses, gorgeant
Ma gueule des bathes délices
De ton jeune foutre astringent,

Ou mordant d'un con à la taille
Juste de tel passe-partout
Mon vit point très gros, mais canaille
Depuis les couilles jusqu'au bout,

Dans la pinette et la minette
Tu tords ton cul d'une façon
Qui n'est pas d'une femme honnête;
Et, nom de Dieu, t'as bien raison!

Tu me fais des langues fourrées,
Quand nous baisons, d'une longueur,
Et d'une ardeur démesurées
Qui me vont, merde! au droit du cœur,

Et ton con exprime ma pine
Comme un ours tetterait un pis,
Ours bien léché, toison rupine
Que la mienne a pour fier tapis.

Ours bien léché: gourmande et soûle,
Ma langue ici peut l'attester
Qui fit à ton clitoris boule-
De-gomme à ne le plus compter.

6   To Madame * * *

When you wrap thighs around my head
And hug, or squeeze them round my bum,
Cramming my craw with a great spread
Of your astringent youthful come,

Or taking with your glistening slot
(Just made for master keys) a nip
Out of my bud (that's all I've got,
But randy right from balls to tip),

Fucking or sucking, there's a twist
You give your arse—and what a gift!—
That decent ladies have all missed:
By God, you've reason in that rift!

And when we kiss, your tongue takes on
Such long and penetrating parts
So ardently that (shit!) it's gone
Straight down into my heart of hearts,

And your quim drains my white liqueur
As a bear milks its mother's dug—
A cub well-licked, with such rich fur
My own rolls on it for a rug:

Licked into shape—my tongue, old soak
And glutton, swears it's long lost count
Of hours spent playing, stroke by stroke,
The cough-sweet game beneath the Mount:

Bien léché, oui, mais âpre en diable,
Ton con joli, taquin, coquin,
Qui rit rouge sur fond de sable:
Telles les lèvres d'Arlequin.

7   Vas unguentatum

Admire la brèche moirée
Et le ton rose-blanc qu'y met
La trace encor de mon entrée
Au Paradis de Mahomet.

Vois, avec un plaisir d'artiste,
O mon vieux regard fatigué
D'ordinaire à bon droit si triste,
Ce spectacle opulent et gai,

Dans un mol écrin de peluche
Noire aux reflets de cuivre roux
Qui serpente comme une ruche,
D'un bijou, le dieu des bijoux,

Well-licked, yes—bitter, though, and grim
That red laugh cut in your brown skin,
Your pretty, teasing, cheeky quim:
So like the lips of Harlequin.

7   Anointed vessel

Admire the watered silky gap,
Mahomet's paradise, that shows
My creamy entry through the lap
Of luxuries that once were rose.

Oh, tired old eyes, take up delight
As painters do, forget your tears
Though warranted, in this rich sight—
This vessel that uplifts and cheers:

In a soft box of plushy fluff,
Black, but with glints of copper-red
And edges crinkly like a ruff,
Lies the great god of gems in bed,

Palpitant de sève et de vie
Et vers l'extase de l'amant
Essorant la senteur ravie,
On dirait, à chaque élément.

Surtout contemple, et puis respire
Et finalement baise encor
Et toujours la gemme en délire,
Le rubis qui rit, fleur du for

Intérieur, tout petit frère
Epris de l'autre et le baisant
Aussi souvent qu'il peut le faire,
Comme lui soufflant à présent . . .

Mais repose-toi, car tu flambes.
Aussi, lui, comment s'apaiser,
Cuisses et ventre, seins et jambes
Qui ne cessez de l'embraser?

Hélas! voici que son ivresse
Me gagne et s'en vient embrasser
Toute ma chair qui se redresse . . .
Allons, c'est à recommencer!

Throbbing with sap and life, and sends
In wafts the best news ever sent,
A perfume his ecstatic friends
Think stolen from each element.

But contemplate this temple, cont-
emplate, then get your breath, and kiss
The jewel having fits in front,
The ruby grinning for its bliss,

Flower of the inner court, kid brother
So mad about the taller one
It kisses till they both half-smother
And puff, then pulse, in unison . . .

But rest; you're blazing now; relax.
It too should calm and cool; but rest?—
In those embrasures and hot cracks
Of thigh and belly, breast and breast?

No, soon its swaying tipsiness
Wins my parts over to a man.
My flesh stands up and nods: right dress!
Begin again where we began!

La galopine
A pleine main
Branle la pine
Au beau gamin.

L'heureux potache
Décalotté
Jouit et crache
De tout côté.

L'enfant, rieuse,
A voir ce lait
Et curieuse
De ce qu'il est,

Hume une goutte
Au bord du pis,
Puis dame! en route,
Ma foi, tant pis!

Pourlèche et baise
Le joli bout,
Plus ne biaise,
Pompe le tout!

Petit vicomte
De Je-ne-sais,
Point ne raconte
Trop ce succès,

The teenage girl's
Extended hand
Palms and unfurls
His fair young stand.

The lucky stiff,
With foreskin drawn,
Comes in a jiff,
Spitting out spawn.

The child laughs, seeing
This singular cream—
Can he be peeing
This jerky stream?—

And sips a drop
From near the tit,
Then, wow, can't stop,
She's off, that's it!

Kisses and licks
The pretty crest,
At that point sticks,
Pumps dry the rest.

Oh, little Lord
Thingummyjig,
Mind no one's bored
With your first frig,

Fleur d'élégances,
Oaristys
De tes vacances
Quatre-vingt-dix:

Ces algarades
Dans les châteaux,
Tes camarades,
Même lourdeaux,

Pourraient sans peine
T'en raconter
A la douzaine
Sans inventer;

Et les cousines,
Anges déchus,
De ces cuisines
Et de ces jus

Sont coutumières,
Pauvres trognons,
Dès leurs premières
Communions:

Ce, jeunes frères,
En attendant
Leurs adultères
Vous impendant.

Your idyll of
The 'ninety vac,
The elegant love
Who kissed you back:

Think how your friends
All wet their tassels
In happy ends
To raids on castles.

They could tell more;
Even the dense
Know how to score—
And none invents.

Their cousin-angels
(Fallen, of course)
Know all the angles
On tubes of sauce.

Poor ducks, they've known
Since first communion
What horn is blown
For family union:

And brothers know
The horns are theirs,
Till time to sow
Others, in pairs.

L'apprenti point trop maigrelet, quinze ans, pas beau,
Gentil dans sa rudesse un peu molle, la peau
Mate, l'œil vif et creux, sort de sa cotte bleue,
Fringante et raide au point, sa déjà grosse queue
Et pine la patronne, une grosse encor bien,
Pâmée au bord du lit dans quel maintien vaurien,
Jambes en l'air et seins au clair, avec un geste!
A voir le gars serrer les fesses sous sa veste
Et les fréquents pas en avant que ses pieds font,
Il appert qu'il n'a pas peur de planter profond
Ni d'enceinter la bonne dame qui s'en fiche
(Son cocu n'est-il pas là, confiant et riche?).
Aussi bien, arrivée au suprême moment,
Elle s'écrie en un subit ravissement:
«Tu m'as fait un enfant, je le sens, et t'en aime
D'autant plus.»—«Et voilà les bonbons du baptême!»
Dit-elle, après la chose; et, tendre, à croppetons,
Lui soupèse et pelote et baise les roustons.

9   Low scene

The apprentice—fifteen, ugly, not too thin,
Nice in a softish uncouth way, dull skin,
Bright deep-set eyes—blue overalls—pulls out
His springy, stiff, well-tuned, quite man-sized spout
And rams the boss's wife—big but still good,
Flopped on the bed's edge—what an attitude!—
Legs up, breasts out, one hand parting her placket.
To see him crush her arse under his jacket
And quickstep forward more than back, it's clear
He's not afraid how deep he plants his gear
Or if the lady fruits—she doesn't care—
Isn't her trusty cuckold always there?—
So when she reaches, as he shoots his goal,
That rapture of the body as a whole,
She cries, 'You've made a child, I feel it, love,
And love you more', and after his last shove
Adds, 'Look, the christening sweets', and squats and tries
To heft and kiss his bollocks through his flies.

Ma petite compatriote,
M'est avis que veniez ce soir
Frapper à ma porte et me voir.
O la scandaleuse ribote
De gros baisers—et de petits,
Conforme à mes gros appétits!
Mais les vôtres sont-ils si mièvres?
Primo, je baiserai vos lèvres,
Toutes! C'est mon cher entremets,
Et les manières que j'y mets,
Comme en toutes choses vécues,
Sont friandes et convaincues.
Vous passerez vos doigts jolis
Dans ma flave barbe d'apôtre
Et je caresserai la vôtre,
Et sur votre gorge de lys,
Où mes ardeurs mettront des roses,
Je poserai ma bouche en feu;
Mes bras se piqueront au jeu,
Pâmés autour de bonnes choses
De dessous la taille et plus bas,—
Puis mes mains, non sans fols combats
Avec vos mains mal courroucées,
Flatteront de tendres fessées

My little countrywoman,
I rather think you'll come and
Knock on my door tonight:
A scandalous pub-crawl
Around the body, all
The drinking-holes in sight,
And some that aren't—you know
My appetite is low?
Well, you're not finicky!
So first your lips—all six—
My favourite savoury—
Taken in dainty licks,
Shall grace my gourmet tongue:
Tongues never shrink among
The things they find in drawers!
Your pretty hands will push
Through my Pale Shepherd's bush
And I'll be stroking yours.
Then on your Lily-breast
I'll kiss hot roses, rest
My burning mouth, and kiss.
My arms will warm to this
Though fainting where they go
Round such good things below—
A lot below—your waist,
Until my hands are placed
Where crazy fingers play
At fighting mine away—
So cross, though tenderly
I flatter with each smack
That beauty of a crack.

Ce beau derrière qu'étreindra
Tout l'effort qui lors bandera
Ma gravité vers votre centre . . .
A mon tour je frappe. O dis: Entre!

11   Pour Rita

J'abomine une femme maigre,
Pourtant je t'adore, ô Rita,
Avec tes lèvres un peu nègre
Où la luxure s'empâta,

Avec tes noirs cheveux, obscènes
A force d'être beaux ainsi,
Et tes yeux où ce sont des scènes
Sentant, parole! le roussi,

Tant leur feu sombre et gai quand même
D'une si lubrique gaîté
Eclaire de grâce suprême
Dans la pire impudicité,

Regard flûtant au virtuose
Es-pratiques dont on se tait:
«Quoi que tu te proposes, ose
Tout ce que ton cul te dictait»;

Now carnal gravity
That hugs you in so tight
Is pulling me upright
And up towards your centre.
I'm knocking now. Say: Enter!

11   For Rita

I loathe thin women with lean hips,
Yet Rita, you I venerate:
Those slightly negro swollen lips
Where lust has made you put on weight!

That hair, so black and beautiful
It's just indecent, and those eyes
Where something gleams in a dark pool
And scents of burning seem to rise,

Eyes hot and gloomy in a face
Gay with a lecherous gaiety,
Flashing out with a saving grace
On the disgraceful things they see,

A look that pipes to all old hands
At habits no-one talks about:
'Dare to do as your arse commands;
Whatever you project, bring out.'

Et sur ta taille comme d'homme,
Fine et très fine cependant,
Ton buste, perplexe Sodome
Entreprenant puis hésitant,

Car dans l'étoffe trop tendue
De tes corsages corrupteurs
Tes petits seins durs de statue
Disent: «Homme ou femme?» aux bandeurs,

Mais tes jambes, que féminine
Leur grâce grasse vers le haut
Jusques aux fesses que devine
Mon désir, jamais en défaut,

Dans les plis cochons de ta robe
Qu'un art salop sut disposer
Pour montrer plus qu'il ne dérobe
Un ventre où le mien se poser!

Bref, tout ton être ne respire
Que faims et soifs et passions . . .
Or je me crois encore pire:
Faudrait que nous comparassions.

Allons, vite au lit, mon infante,
Çà, livrons-nous jusqu'au matin
Une bataille triomphante
A qui sera le plus putain.

And on your waist that's like a man's
(A smart waist, very smart), that bust!—
Which Sodom stares at in a trance,
Rousing, then sitting on his lust:

In the tight cloth of bodices
That tempt, deceive, and may protect,
Your small breasts, statue-hard, say, 'Guess:
Woman or man?' to the erect.

Ah, but your legs—how feminine
Their grace that spreads and gaining height
Opens where buttocks first begin,
Glimpsed by my prurience, always right,

Among your dress's bawdy folds
Arranged by a design so lewd
It offers, more than it withholds,
A belly on which mine can brood.

In short, all of you breathes an air
Of passionate hunger and bad thirst,
Which I advise you to compare
With mine, as I think mine the worst.

So quick, let's go to no man's land—
There, princess: bed, this battleground
Where both sides win and nothing's banned;
Let's see who's randier all round.

Un rêve de cuisses de femmes
Ayant pour ciel et pour plafond
Les culs et les cons de ces dames,
Très beaux, qui viennent et qui vont

Dans un ballon de jupes gaies
Sur des airs gentils et cochons;
Et les culs vous ont de ces raies,
Et les cons vous ont des manchons!

Des bas blancs sur quels mollets fermes
Si rieurs et si bandatifs
Avec, en haut, sans fins ni termes,
Ce train d'appas en pendentifs,

Et des bottines bien cambrées
Moulant des pieds grands juste assez
Mènent des danses mesurées
En pas vifs, comme un peu lassés.

Une sueur particulière
Sentant à la fois bon et pas,
Foutre et mouille, et trouduculière,
Et haut de cuisse, et bas de bas,

Flotte et vire, joyeuse et molle,
Mêlée à des parfums de peau
A nous rendre la tête folle
Que les youtres ont sans chapeau.

I'm in a dream of women's thighs:
No ceilings there, no walls around;
The bums of ladies fill the skies
And quims fly past without a sound.

Ballooning skirts of coloured stuffs
Float in on nice and bawdy airs,
The cunts all showing off their muffs,
The buttocks how they part in pairs.

White stockings on firm calves suspend
This gallery of charming loins
Smiling above me without end
On the pendentives of their groins.

And little boots that shape just right
The arching fronts of little feet
Dance to quick measures, with a slight
Drag, as if tired, on the beat.

A rather special sweat is smelt
Just here, not bad, but rather high,
Of come and damp and human pelt
And stocking-foot and top of thigh,

The sloppy, happy scents that mix
With all the perfumes of our laps
And mock the self-control of pricks,
Even the kind that still wear caps.

Notez combien bonne ma place
Se trouve dans ce bal charmant:
Je suis par terre, et ma surface
Semble propice apparemment

Aux appétissantes danseuses
Qui veulent bien, on dirait pour
Telles intentions farceuses,
Tournoyer sur moi, quand mon tour,

Ce, par un extraordinaire
Privilège en elles ou moi,
Sans me faire mal, au contraire!
Car l'aimable, le doux émoi

Que ces cinq cent mille chatouilles
De petons vous caracolant
A même les jambes, les couilles,
Le ventre, la queue et le gland!

Les chants se taisent et les danses
Cessent. Aussitôt les fessiers
De mettre au pas leurs charmes denses.
O ciel! l'un d'entre eux, tu t'assieds

Juste sur ma face, de sorte
Que ma langue entre les deux trous
Divins, vague de porte en porte
Au pourchas de riches ragoûts.

Tous les derrières à la file
S'en viennent généreusement
M'apporter, chacun en son style,
Ce vrai banquet d'un vrai gourmand.

Please note the perfect place I've found
For sitting out this ball of dreams:
My lucky body on the ground
Is a fine dancing-floor, it seems—

In turn each appetizing girl
That dances takes a turn on me.
They mean it as a joke, and twirl
Across my navel pointedly,

But by some harmless miracle
Arranged for me, or else for them,
Their lovely joke is practical:
How sweet that flutter at my stem!

The tickle of their tiny feet
That bounce and caper as they stand
On belly, legs, and where they meet,
My balls, my tail, my favourite gland!

The music stops; the dancing too.
The buttock-bearers on the spot
Angle their charms into a queue.
Oh heavens: one of them, guess what?

Sits on my face, so that my tongue,
The scholar's organ, can peruse
Both holy subjects there, among
Aromas of their home-made stews.

All the behinds in Indian file
Come on then generously to feed
Each in an individual style
The true discriminating greed.

Je me réveille, je me touche;
C'est bien moi, le pouls au galop . . .
Le nom de Dieu de fausse couche!
Le nom de Dieu de vrai salop!

13 Reddition

Je suis foutu. Tu m'as vaincu.
Je n'aime plus que ton gros cu
Tant baisé, léché, reniflé,
Et que ton cher con tant branlé,
Piné—car je ne suis pas l'homme
Pour Gomorrhe ni pour Sodome,
Mais pour Paphos et pour Lesbos
(Et tant gamahuché, ton con),
Converti par tes seins si beaux,
Tes seins lourds que mes mains soupèsent
Afin que mes lèvres les baisent
Et, comme l'on hume un flacon,
Sucent leurs bouts raides, puis mous,
Ainsi qu'il nous arrive à nous
Avec nos gaules variables.
C'est un plaisir de tous les diables

I wake. I touch myself. It's me.
It's me, with racing pulse. Oh God!
The dream was wet. Unless it's pee.
Oh bloody hell, you dirty sod!

13 Surrender

I'm fucked. Yes, I capitulate.
Now I love nothing but your great
Posterior with its friendly rift
So often kissed and licked and sniffed
And your dear cunt so often stirred
By joysticks felt and even heard.
I'm not the man I was—you'll find
I've left those circles far behind,
And Sodom and Gomorrah lose
What Paphos may be glad to use,
And Lesbos—for I know your cunt
Finds gamarooshing no affront—
Converted by the softer cleft
Between these heavy breasts I heft
And lift like flasks to my pursed lips,
For kisses, little nuzzling sips
At their first stiff then drooping tips—
Don't worry, we can make them swell:
Sometimes our pricks go down as well.
Oh marvellous, having it away
Beneath you in the Roman way—

Que tirer un coup en gamin,
En épicier ou en levrette,
Ou à la Marie-Antoinette
Et cætera jusqu'à demain
Avec toi, despote adorée,
Dont la volonté m'est sacrée,
Plaisir infernal qui me tue
Et dans lequel je m'exténue
A satisfaire ta luxure.
Le foutre s'épand de mon vit
Comme le sang d'une blessure . . .
N'importe! Tant que mon cœur vit
Et que palpite encor mon être,
Je veux remplir en tout ta loi,
N'ayant, dure maîtresse, en toi
Plus de maîtresse, mais un maître.

14   Régals

Croise tes cuisses sur ma tête
De façon à ce que ma langue,
Taisant toute sotte harangue,
Ne puisse plus que faire fête

Inch up, or turn the other cheek,
And try a second round in Greek—
Like English missionaries, like dogs,
In bed, or in the bath like frogs,
Like Marie Antoinette on swings
Fitted with those Far Eastern things,
And so forth through the night with you,
Tyrant adored in all I do:
Though answering your sacred will
Gives me such pleasure it can kill
And leaves me gasping as I thrust
To satisfy your pangs of lust.
At last the come comes welling out
Like blood in a half-hearted gout . . .
No matter! While I'm on the job
And something's left in me to throb,
I wish my tool to be correct
And keep the law as you direct,
As if, hard mistress, I instead
Had a hard master in my bed.

14   Treats

Cross, cross your thighs around
My interesting head
And make my tongue instead
Of boring you with sound
Come boring in to sup.

A ton con ainsi qu'à ton cu
Dont je suis l'à-jamais vaincu
Comme de tout ton corps, du reste,
Et de ton âme mal céleste,
Et de ton esprit carnassier
Qui dévore en moi l'idéal
Et m'a fait le plus putassier
Du plus pur, du plus lilial
Que j'étais avant ta rencontre
Depuis des ans et puis des ans.
Là, dispose-toi bien et montre
Par quelques gestes complaisants
Qu'au fond t'aimes ton vieux bonhomme
Ou du moins le souffres faisant
Minette (avec boule de gomme)
Et feuille de rose, tout comme
Un plus jeune mieux séduisant
Sans doute, mais moins bath en somme
Quant à la science et au faire.
O ton con! qu'il sent bon! j'y fouille
Tant de la gueule que du blaire
Et j'y fais le diable et j'y flaire
Et j'y farfouille et j'y bafouille
Et j'y renifle et oh! j'y bave
Dans ton con à l'odeur cochonne
Que surplombe une motte flave
Et qu'un duvet roux environne

It loves to be shut up.
I love to be the guest
Of cunt and arse (and breast),
The prisoner of your whole
Young body and your soul.
It's such fun in your nick
With all these heavenly screws
So fond (and full) of juice
You've eaten up the prick
Of conscience I had once.
You lovely carnivore!—
And I'd been Lily-pure
For months and months and months!
Well, there; spread out; unbend;
By some caressing move
Show in the end you love
Your old man in the end.
At least, you let him come
The bonbon pussy trick
And the rose-petal lick
That floats from quim to bum,
As much as if it were
One younger, handsomer
Than me, though not as great
On what and how to mate.
Oh, marvellous smells of cunt!
I dive into your front
Gob first, which somewhat muffles
The snuffling in your ruffles
As chin and tongue and snout
Slaver and root about.
There is a mousey mound
With fluffy red around
Which overhangs a well

Qui mène au trou miraculeux,
Où je farfouille, où je bafouille,
Où je renifle et où je bave
Avec le soin méticuleux
Et l'âpre ferveur d'un esclave
Affranchi de tout préjugé.
La raie adorable que j'ai
Léchée *amoroso* depuis
Les reins en passant par le puits
Où je m'attarde en un long stage
Pour les dévotions d'usage,
Me conduit tout droit à la fente
Triomphante de mon infante.
Là, je dis un salamalec
Absolument ésotérique
Au clitoris rien moins que sec,
Si bien que ma tête d'en bas
Qu'exaspèrent tous ces ébats
S'épanche en blanche rhétorique,
Mais s'apaise dès ces prémisses

Et je m'endors entre tes cuisses
Qu'à travers tout cet émoi tendre
La fatigue t'a fait détendre.

Where your good odours dwell.
In this miraculous furrow
I splutter, grope and burrow
As anxious and precise
As any slave who fills
The norms of others' wills,
And never thinks: 'Not nice.'
The parting I adore so
Has been well licked: I waste
No time too near the waist.
Andante amoroso
I'm soon at that first hole
But stay there rather long
Devoting heart and soul
To holy evensong.
And then on down the track
To your triumphant crack,
My princess, where I do
A deep kowtow or two,
And give my secret kiss
To your wet clitoris.
All this linguistic stuff
Maddens my other head:
Far off, it's had enough
And says so on the bed
With much white rhetoric.
A half-cock, rather thick
Conclusion, but it's pleased.
And as fatigue unties
The knot where pleasure's squeezed,
I sleep between your thighs.

Depuis que ce m'est plus commode
De baiser en gamin, j'adore
Cette manière et l'aime encore
Plus quand j'applique la méthode

Qui consiste à mettre mes mains
Bien fort sur ton bon gros cul frais,
Chatouille un peu conçue exprès
Pour mieux entrer dans tes chemins.

Alors ma queue est en ribote
De ce con, qui, de fait, la baise,
Et de ce ventre qui lui pèse
D'un poids salop—et ça clapote,

Et les tétons de déborder
De la chemise lentement
Et de danser indolemment,
Et mes yeux de comme bander,

Tandis que les tiens, d'une vache,
Tels ceux-là des Junons antiques,
Leur fichent des regards obliques,
Profonds comme des coups de hache,

Si que je suis magnétisé
Et que mon cabochon d'en bas,
Non toutefois sans quels combats!
Se rend tout à fait médusé.

15   The way the ladies ride

Now I no longer kneel to you
But serve you upwards, I adore
This way—riding St George; still more
If (just a twist upon the screw)

My hands, placed firmly, can contain
The nice swing of your big cool arse,
Tickling the slipways so I pass
Easily up the wringing lane.

This starts my prick's head going round,
Drunk on your deeply kissing cunt
And belly grinding down so blunt
And messy, with a slapping sound.

And now your paps begin to slop
Out of your nightdress by degrees
And indolently dance at ease,
While my eyes try to stand, and pop

Towards your eyes which, blank as stone,
Like ox-eyed Hera of the Greeks
Look back askance down level cheeks
With glances cutting to the bone,

Till under your hypnotic sway
My pendent jewel on its pole,
Overcome by the better hole,
Stands still, quite petrified, at bay:

Et je jouis et je décharge
Dans ce vrai cauchemar de viande
A la fois friande et gourmande
Et tour à tour étroite et large,

Et qui remonte et redescend
Et rebondit sur mes roustons
En sauts où mon vit à tâtons
Pris d'un vertige incandescent

Parmi des foutres et des mouilles
Meurt, puis revit, puis meurt encore,
Revit, remeurt, revit encore
Par tout ce foutre et que de mouilles!

Cependant que mes doigts, non sans
Te faire un tas de postillons,
Légers comme des papillons
Mais profondément caressants,

Et que mes paumes, de tes fesses
Froides modérément tout juste
Remontent *lento* vers le buste
Tiède sous leurs chaudes caresses.

And I come pouring out inside
That incubus of solid meat
That daintily craves cock to eat,
That sweet small slit now gaping wide

And lifting up and dropping back
To land on bollocks with a bump,
And bouncing where my white-hot stump
Dizzily feeling round the crack

Among the juices and the come
Dies and revives and dies again,
Retools, and dies, and tools again,
Through so much juice and all that come.

My fingers meanwhile, which full-pelt
Were tapping light quick commentaries
On your unguarded orifice,
Butterflies, but profoundly felt,

Leave the glen slowly for their calm
Long climb from buttocks' moderate chill
Around toward each tremulous hill,
Warm in the hot and hollowed palm.

Je suis couché tout de mon long sur son lit frais:
Il fait grand jour; c'est plus cochon, plus fait exprès,
Par le prolongement dans la lumière crue
De la fête nocturne immensément accrue,
Pour la persévérance et la rage du cu
Et ce soin de se faire soi-même cocu.
Elle est à poils et s'accroupit sur mon visage
Pour se faire gamahucher, car je fus sage
Hier et c'est—bonne, elle, au-delà du penser!—
Sa royale façon de me récompenser.
Je dis royale, je devrais dire divine:
Ces fesses, chair sublime, alme peau, pulpe fine,
Galbe puissamment pur, blanc, riche, aux stries d'azur,
Cette raie au parfum bandatif, rose-obscur,
Lente, grasse, et le puits d'amour, que dire sur!
Régal final, dessert du con bouffé, délire
De ma langue harpant les plis comme une lyre!
Et ces fesses encor, telle une lune en deux
Quartiers, mystérieuse et joyeuse, où je veux
Dorénavant nicher mes rêves de poète
Et mon cœur de tendeur et mes rêves d'esthète!
Et, maîtresse, ou mieux, maître en silence obéi,
Elle trône sur moi, caudataire ébloui.

I'm lying full length on her cool divan.
Broad day: that's bawdier, better for our plan
(Because we've kept up all the joys of night,
Enlarging them immensely by raw light)
For the loins' perseverance, the well-hung
Rage to be cuckolded by one's own tongue.
She's naked and she crouches on my face
For gamarooshing now because she says
Yesterday I behaved, and so she thanks
And royally contents the supine ranks.
No, the content's divine: those buttocks hover,
Sublime flesh, fine pulp showing through their cover
Of rich white streaked with blue, curves pure and strong,
The crack with dark pink scents that make you long
To be where you belong, slow-burning, fat,
The well of love, the never well-dressed twat,
Dessert of full-gorged cunt, the treat of treats
To this tongue madly harping in the pleats,
And still those buttocks, a half-moon that splits
In two mysterious and joyful bits,
Where now my dreams will always nest, to warm
My poacher's heart, my thoughts of abstract form.
And so, well-served, my mistress—master!—sits
On speechless, dazzled, me: a throne that fits.

Morale en raccourci

Une tête de blonde et de grâce pâmée,
Sous un cou roucouleur de beaux tétons bandants,
Et leur médaillon sombre à la mamme enflammée,
Ce buste assis sur des coussins bas, cependant
Qu'entre deux jambes, très vibrantes, très en l'air,
Une femme à genoux vers quels soins occupée—
Amour le sait—ne montre aux dieux que l'épopée
Candide de son cul splendide, miroir clair
De la Beauté qui veut s'y voir afin d'y croire.
Cul féminin, vainqueur serein du cul viril,
Fût-il éphébéen, et fût-il puéril,
Cul féminin, cul sur tous culs, los, culte et gloire!

A brief moral

A golden head, head of a fainting grace;
Below a throat that purrs, outstanding paps
With dark medallions and stiff glowing caps—
This bust disposed in a low, cushioned place;
While in between two legs that lift and beat,
A woman on her knees—Love only knows
What service she attends—to heaven shows
The artless epic of her shining seat,
Beauty's clear mirror, where she loves to gaze,
See and believe herself. O woman's arse,
Roundly defeating man's in every class,
O arse of arses: Glory! Worship! Praise!

Hombres

Men

O ne blasphème pas, poète; et souviens-toi.
Certes la femme est bien, elle vaut qu'on la baise,
Son cul lui fait honneur, encor qu'un brin obèse,
Et je l'ai savouré maintes fois, quant à moi.

Ce cul (et les tétons), quel nid à nos caresses!
Je l'embrasse à genoux et lèche son pertuis
Tandis que mes doigts vont, fouillant dans l'autre puits,
Et les beaux seins, combien cochonnes leurs paresses!

Et puis, il sert, ce cul, encor, surtout au lit
Comme adjuvant aux fins de coussins, de sous-ventre,
De ressort à boudin du vrai ventre pour qu'entre
Plus avant l'homme dans la femme qu'il élit.

J'y délasse mes mains, mes bras aussi, mes jambes,
Mes pieds.—Tant de fraîcheur, d'élastique rondeur
M'en font un reposoir désirable où, rôdeur,
Par instants le désir sautille en vœux ingambes.

Mais comparer le cul de l'homme à ce bon cu,
A ce gros cul moins voluptueux que pratique,
Le cul de l'homme, fleur de joie et d'esthétique,
Surtout l'en proclamer le serf et le vaincu,

«C'est mal», a dit l'Amour. Et la voix de l'Histoire:
«Cul de l'homme, honneur pur de l'Hellade et décor
Divin de Rome vraie et plus divin encor,
De Sodome morte, martyre pour sa gloire.

I   'Now, poet, don't be sacrilegious . . .'

Now, poet, don't be sacrilegious: think a bit.
Women are fine, well worth a kiss—and more than that!
Their arses do them credit, though a pinch too fat,
Which I have often tried and relished, I admit.

That arse (and tits), ah, what a nest for our caress!
I clasp it kneeling, and then lick its puncture, while
My fingers dabble in the other moist defile
Or tease the fine breasts' loose and lecherous laziness.

It serves as well, that arse, specially for bed effects,
For tilting holy places to a higher plane,
Helping a man, like cushions, like a spring, to gain
A deeper purchase in the woman he elects.

I rest my hands, my arms too, on these bouncy spheres—
And legs, and feet—a lovely halt upon the rounds,
Whose cool repeated curve has lust, in leaps and bounds,
Popping right up again with sprightlier ideas.

But to compare the arse of man to this good bum,
This coarse posterior less for pleasure than for use
To the male buttocks, joy of joys and view of views—
Much less claim ours a vassal it has overcome—

'Now that's not good,' says Eros. And hear History's voice:
'The arse of man—to Greece, pure honour; to true Rome,
Divinely fitting charm; diviner still at home
In Sodom, glorious martyr to its glorious choice.

Shakespeare, abandonnant du coup Ophélia,
Cordélia, Desdémona, tout son beau sexe
Chantait en vers magnificents—qu'un sot s'en vexe—
La forme masculine et son alleluia.

Les Valois étaient fous du mâle et dans notre ère
L'Europe embourgeoisée et féminine tant
Néanmoins admira ce Louis de Bavière,
Le roi vierge au grand cœur pour l'homme seul battant.

La Chair, même, la chair de la femme proclame
Le cul, le vit, le torse et l'œil du fier Puceau,
—Et c'est pourquoi, d'après le conseil à Rousseau,
Il faut parfois, poète, un peu «quitter la dame».

1891

'And Shakespeare dropped at last the heroines of his plays,
Ophelia and the others, all her lovely sex,
To write magnificent verse—only a fool objects—
On manly beauty that he loved and wished to praise.

'The Valois kings were mad for maleness, and since then
Our Europe, now grown female, soft, and middle-class,
Still admired Ludwig, Wagner's and Bavaria's,
That virgin king whose great heart only beat for men.

'The Flesh itself (a woman's!) always has implied
The arse, the cock, the chest, the eye of the Proud Youth . . .'
—And, poet, that is why, in line with Rousseau's truth,
One sometimes ought to 'leave the ladies on one side'.

Mes amants n'appartiennent pas aux classes riches:
Ce sont des ouvriers faubouriens ou ruraux,
Leurs quinze et leurs vingt ans sans apprêts sont mal chiches
De force assez brutale et de procédés gros.

Je les goûte en habits de travail, cotte et veste;
Ils ne sentent pas l'ambre et fleurent de santé
Pure et simple; leur marche un peu lourde, va, preste
Pourtant, car jeune, et grave en l'élasticité;

Leurs yeux francs et matois crépitent de malice
Cordiale et des mots naïvement rusés
Partent non sans un gai juron qui les épice
De leur bouche bien fraîche aux solides baisers;

Leur pine vigoureuse et leurs fesses joyeuses
Réjouissent la nuit et ma queue et mon cu;
Sous la lampe et le petit jour, leurs chairs joyeuses
Ressuscitent mon désir las, jamais vaincu.

Cuisses, âmes, mains, tout mon être pêle-mêle,
Mémoire, pieds, cœur, dos et l'oreille et le nez,
Et la fressure, tout gueule une ritournelle
Et trépigne un chahut dans leurs bras forcenés.

Un chahut, une ritournelle, fol et folle,
Et plutôt divins qu'infernals, plus infernals
Que divins, à m'y perdre et j'y nage et j'y vole,
Dans leur sueur et leur haleine, dans ces bals.

2 A thousand and three

My lovers come, not from the floating classes: they're
Labourers from the depths of suburbs or the land,
Aged fifteen, twenty, with no graces, but an air
Of pretty brutal strength and manners none too grand.

I like them in their work-clothes—jacket, overalls:
Smelling of pure and simple health, never a whiff
Of scent: their step sounds heavy, yes, but still it falls
Nimbly enough—they're young, their bounce a little stiff.

Their crafty and wide eyes crackle with cordial
Mischief: the wit of their naïvely knowing quips
Comes salted with gay swearwords, to be rhythmical,
From their fresh, wholesome mouths and soundly kissing lips;

With energetic knobs and buttockfuls of joy
They can rejoice my arsehole and my cock all night;
By lamplight and at dawn their flesh, all over joy,
Wakes my desire again, tired but still full of fight.

Thighs, hands, and souls, all of me mixed up, memory, feet,
Heart, back and ear and nose and all my ringing guts
Begin to bawl in chorus as they hit the beat,
Reeling and jig-a-jigging in their frenzied ruts:

A crazy dance, a crazy chorus as we're lined
Up, up, divinely rising because hell is high
On heavenly routes: I dance to save myself, and find,
Swimming in sweat, it's in our common breath I fly.

Mes deux Charles: l'un, jeune tigre aux yeux de chatte,
Sorte d'enfant de chœur grandissant en soudard;
L'autre, fier gaillard, bel effronté que n'épate
Que ma pente vertigineuse vers son dard.

Odilon, un gamin, mais monté comme un homme,
Ses pieds aiment les miens épris de ses orteils
Mieux encor, mais pas plus que de son reste en somme
Adorable drûment, mais ses pieds non pareils!

Caresseurs, satin frais, délicates phalanges
Sous les plantes, autour des chevilles et sur
La cambrure veineuse, et ces baisers étranges
Si doux, de quatre pieds ayant une âme, sûr!

Antoine, encor? proverbial quant à la queue,
Lui, mon roi triomphal et mon suprême Dieu,
Taraudant tout mon cœur de sa prunelle bleue,
Et tout mon cul de son épouvantable épieu;

Paul, un athlète blond aux pectoraux superbes,
Poitrine blanche aux durs boutons sucés ainsi
Que le bon bout; François souple comme des gerbes:
Ses jambes de danseur, et beau, son chibre aussi!

Auguste qui se fait de jour en jour plus mâle
(Il était bien joli quand ça nous arriva);
Jules, un peu putain avec sa beauté pâle;
Henri, miraculeux conscrit qui, las! s'en va;

Et vous tous! à la file ou confondus, en bande
Ou seuls, vision si nette des jours passés,
Passions du présent, futur qui croît et bande,
Chéris sans nombre qui n'êtes jamais assez!

1891

So, my two Charleses: one, young tiger with cat's eyes,
A choirboy with his volume swelling rough and thick;
The other a wild blade so cheeky I surprise
Him only with my dizzy penchant for his prick;

And Odilon, a kid, equipped, though, like a lord:
His feet in love with mine, which rave about their catch—
Those toes!—though thick and fast the rest of him's adored—
Those feet!—there's nothing like them!—even they don't match!

How they caress, so satin cool, with sensitive
Knuckles that stroke the soles and, round the ankles, graze
Over the veiny arch! how these strange kisses give
A sweet soul to this quadruped with soulful ways!

Then Antoine, with that tail of legendary size,
My god, my phallocrat who triumphs from the rear,
Piercing my heart with the blue lightning of his eyes,
My violet arsehole with his terrifying spear;

Paul, a blond athlete—pectorals that you could eat!—
A white breast with hard buttons that are sucked as much
As the more juicy end; and François, lithe as wheat,
His pecker coiled in that fantastic dancer's crutch;

Auguste, who daily makes himself more masculine
(Oh when it happened first he was a pretty lass!);
Jules, rather whorish with his pallid beauty's skin;
Henri, the marvellous conscript who's gone off, alas!—

I see you all, alone or friends together, some
Unique, some I confuse, a vision of past love
Clear as my passions who come now, or are to come,
My countless darlings who can never come enough!

3   Balanide

I

C'est un plus petit cœur
Avec la pointe en l'air;
Symbole doux et fier,
C'est un plus tendre cœur.

Il verse ah! que de pleurs
Corrosifs plus que feu,
Prolongés mieux qu'adieu,
Blancs comme blanches fleurs!

Vêtu de violet,
Fait beau le voir yssir,
Mais ô tout le plaisir
Qu'il donne quand lui plaît!

Comme un évêque au chœur
Il est plein d'onction.
Sa bénédiction
Va de l'autel au chœur.

Il ne met que du soir
Au réveil auroral
Son anneau pastoral
D'améthyste et d'or noir.

Puis le rite accompli,
Déchargé congrûment,
De ramener dûment
Son capuce joli.

3   Acornesque

I

A heart, a smaller heart,
Point up—a point that shows
It stands proud for sweet blows:
It's a more tender heart.

It pours out tears for things:
Caustic as fire, they dry
Slower than a goodbye,
White as white blossomings.

Look! it's a lovely sight,
Got up in violet
And sallying forth, all set
To please with all its might—

A bishop in the nave
Brimming with unctuousness,
Whose blessing reaches us
All the way up the nave.

Only from dusk until
The alarming light of dawn
Its pastoral ring is worn:
Dark gold with purple jewel.

Then, service done, a good
Job discharged fittingly,
It bows and decently
Pulls up its pretty hood.

II

Gland, point suprême de l'être
        De mon maître,
De mon amant adoré
Qu'accueille avec joie et crainte
        Ton étreinte,
Mon heureux cul, perforé

Tant et tant par ce gros membre
        Qui se cambre,
Se gonfle et, tout glorieux
De ses hauts faits et prouesses,
        Dans les fesses
Fonce en élans furieux,—

Nourricier de ma fressure,
        Source sûre
Où ma bouche aussi suça,
Gland, ma grande friandise,
        Quoi qu'en dise
Quelque fausse honte, or çà,

Gland, mes délices, viens, dresse
        Ta caresse
De chaud satin violet
Qui dans ma main se harnache
        En panache
Soudain d'opale et de lait.

II

My master's knob, the high-point of
    My lover's love,
Peak of a being that's adored,
That with a joyful, frightened gasp
    My arse can clasp
And welcome, happy to be bored

So many times by that stout prick,
    That stretches, thick
And swelling, boastfully evokes
Its gallantries by field and beach
    And in the breach
Charges with furious bounding strokes—

O root, who feed my guts with sap,
    O upright tap
Where my mouth also sucks and plays,
O delicacy I like best
    Warmly expressed,
Whatever false shame sighs and says—

Come, acorn, come, my heart of oak,
    Sit straight and poke
The hot mauve baton smooth as silk
Into my hand where it arrays
    Itself in sprays
Of sudden opalescent milk.

Ce n'est que pour une douce
    Sur le pouce
Que je t'invoque aujourd'hui
Mais quoi! ton ardeur se fâche . . .
    O moi lâche!
Va, tout à toi, tout à lui,

Ton caprice, règle unique.
    Je rapplique
Pour la bouche et pour le cu:
Les voici tout prêts, en selle,
    D'humeur telle
Qu'il te faut, maître invaincu.

Puis, gland, nectar et dictame
    De mon âme,
Rentre en ton prépuce, lent
Comme un dieu dans son nuage.
    Mon hommage
T'y suit, fidèle—et galant.

1891

I only called you out to come
    Across my thumb
A little jogging wank today:
But now your ardour's roused, of course,
    On its high horse,
Go on, it's all yours, up, away!—

It's bugger's choice, the only rule.
    So to your tool
I re-apply for both my holes,
Ready, side-saddle or astride,
    As you decide,
And willing, master of all souls!

And then, dear knob, my balm, my nectar,
    My soul's erector,
Home to your foreskin; fade away
Slowly as gods in nimbus can.
    For I'm your man:
I'll follow, ever true—and gay.

5   Sur une statue

Eh quoi! dans cette ville d'eaux,
Trêve, repos, paix, intermède,
Encor toi de face ou de dos,
Beau petit ami Ganymède?

L'aigle t'emporte, on dirait comme
A regret, de parmi des fleurs;
Son aile, d'élans économe,
Semble te vouloir par ailleurs

Que chez ce Jupin tyrannique,
Comme qui dirait au Revard
Et son œil qui nous fait la nique
Te coule un drôle de regard.

Bah, reste avec nous, bon garçon,
Notre ennui, viens donc le distraire
Un peu, de la bonne façon.
N'es-tu pas notre petit frère?

Aix-les-Bains, 7bre 89

5   On a statue

What! even in this spa of spas,
Town of truce, rest, peace, interlude,
You again, met full-face or -arse,
Ganymede, pretty friend, still nude!

The eagle lifts you off, I'd say
With some regret, from the flower-bed;
His wings flap grudgingly away
And seem to wish you'd come instead

Up to some dreamy mountain nook
Nearby—not to that tyrant god:
His eye shoots us a narrow look,
With one at you that's really odd.

Hell, stay with us, dear boy—do stay;
Come and divert us; come, distract
Our boredom in the nicest way.
Aren't you our little brother in fact?

6   Rendez-vous

Dans la chambre encore fatale
De l'encor fatale maison
Où la raison et la morale
Le tiennent plus que de raison,

Il semble attendre la venue
A quoi, misère, il ne croit pas,
De quelque présence connue
Et murmure entre haut et bas:

«Ta voix claironne dans mon âme
Et tes yeux flambent dans mon cœur.
Le monde dit que c'est infâme;
Mais que me fait, ô mon vainqueur!

«J'ai la tristesse et j'ai la joie,
Et j'ai l'amour encore un coup,
L'amour ricaneur qui larmoie,
O toi beau comme un petit loup!

«Tu vins à moi, gamin farouche,
C'est toi—joliesse et bagout—
Rusé du corps et de la bouche,
Qui me violentes dans tout

«Mon scrupule envers ton extrême
Jeunesse et ton enfance mal
Encore débrouillée, et même
Presque dans tout mon animal.

6 Meeting

In the still doomed and fatal room
Of the same house still full of fate,
Where reason, and the heart, and doom,
Hold him too long, too long and late,

He waits—it looks like waiting—though
For one he thinks will not appear,
Some presence that he used to know,
And mutters so the room can hear:

'Your voice rings in my spirit still
And in my heart your eyes still glare.
The world says it's unspeakable;
But what do I, your captive, care?

'I have that sadness, that joy too,
And I have love back once again,
Love crying while it laughs at you—
And you, the beauty of young men!

'You came to me, a savage kid;
It was you, pretty, glib, and sly
In all your mouth and body did,
That violated me and my

'Honour, my scruples over your
Extreme youth, with your childhood scarce
Cleared up as yet, then broke and tore
Through me wherever you could pierce.

«Deux, trois ans sont passés à peine,
Suffisants pour viriliser
Ta fleur d'alors et ton haleine
Encore prompte à s'épuiser.

«Quel rude gaillard tu dois être
Et que les instants seraient bons
Si tu pouvais venir! Mais, traître,
Tu promets, tu dis: J'en réponds.

«Tu jures le ciel et la terre,
Puis tu rates les rendez-vous . . .
Ah! cette fois, viens! Obtempère
A mes désirs qui tournent fous.

«Je t'attends comme le Messie,
Arrive, tombe dans mes bras;
Une rare fête choisie
Te guette, arrive, tu verras!»

Du phosphore en ses yeux s'allume
Et sa lèvre au souris pervers
S'agace aux barbes de la plume
Qu'il tient pour écrire ces vers . . .

1891

'Two or three years have passed; that's just
Enough to touch with manly fuzz
The bloom you had, and make your lust
Much better-winded than it was.

'You must be a great strapping tough
By now—the pleasures would be rare
If you could come . . . But false to love,
You promise, you say: Look, I swear,

'You cross your heart and hope to die,
Then you miss every date we've had.
But, this time, come: this time, comply
With my desires: I'm going mad.

'I wait for you to come again,
Like Jesus, to my arms; you'll see
A real feast laid to entertain
Your special choices. Come to me!'

Phosphoric gleams light up his eyes;
His lips twist in a vicious leer
And scratch against the quill he tries
To hold to write the verses here . . .

Monte sur moi comme une femme
Que je baiserais en gamin.
Là. C'est cela. T'es à ta main?
Tandis que mon vit t'entre, lame

Dans du beurre, du moins ainsi
Je puis te baiser sur la bouche,
Te faire une langue farouche
Et cochonne, et si douce, aussi!

Je vois tes yeux auxquels je plonge
Les miens jusqu'au fond de ton cœur
D'où mon désir revient vainqueur
Dans une luxure de songe.

Je caresse le dos nerveux,
Les flancs ardents et frais, la nuque,
La double mignonne perruque
Des aisselles et les cheveux!

Ton cul à cheval sur mes cuisses
Les pénètre de son doux poids
Pendant que s'ébat mon lourdois
Aux fins que tu te réjouisses,

Et tu te réjouis, petit,
Car voici que ta belle gaule,
Jalouse aussi d'avoir son rôle,
Vite, vite gonfle, grandit,

Climb on, as women do to ride
St George, who kisses lying back.
There, that's it. Are you on the track?
While my tool enters your inside

(A blade in butter), now like this
At least my mouth finds yours in range,
And tongues can make their wild exchange,
A randy—sweet and randy—kiss.

This way, I see your eyes, and thrust
Long looks deep in them to your heart
Where desire consummates apart
Its visionary acts of lust.

This way, your wiry back is there
To stroke, your cool and ardent sides,
The dainty double bush that hides
Your armpits, and I stroke your hair!

Your good seat straddling my groins,
Its soft weight sinking firmly on,
Grips as my bucking stallion
Cavorts to entertain your loins,

And you are entertained, as well,
Dear boy, because your handsome prick,
Equally keen to take a trick,
Swiftly grows up and starts to swell

Raidit . . . Ciel! la goutte, la perle
Avant-courrière, vient briller
Au méat rose: l'avaler,
Moi, je le dois, puisque déferle

Le mien de flux. Or c'est mon lot
De faire tôt d'avoir aux lèvres
Ton gland chéri tout lourd de fièvres
Qu'il décharge en un royal flot.

Lait suprême, divin phosphore
Sentant bon la fleur d'amandier,
Où vient l'âpre soif mendier,
La soif de toi qui me dévore.

Mais il va, riche et généreux,
Le don de ton adolescence,
Communiant de ton essence
Tout mon être ivre d'être heureux.

1891

And stiffen . . . Oh my God! the pearl,
The warning drop, comes out to shine
At the pink opening: and it's mine
To gobble, as my own tides curl

And foam in floods. Now it's my luck
To look alive with lips wide spread
For your dear cock whose splitting head
Bursts in the royal flush of fuck—

Prime milk, phosphoric, heavenly dew
That smells of blossoming almond-trees,
Where thirst comes begging on its knees,
My harsh consuming thirst for you.

But it's so rich and generous—
The brimming gift of youth, the real
Presence that you infuse I feel
Right through me, drunk on happiness.

Un peu de merde et de fromage
Ne sont pas pour effaroucher
Mon nez, ma bouche et mon courage
Dans l'amour de gamahucher.

L'odeur m'est assez gaie en somme,
Du trou du cul de mes amants,
Aigre et fraîche comme de pomme
Dans la moiteur de sains ferments.

Et ma langue que rien ne dompte,
Par la douceur des longs poils roux
Raide et folle de bonne honte,
Assouvit là ses plus forts goûts.

Puis, pourléchant le périnée
Et les couilles d'un mode lent,
Au long du chibre contournée
S'arrête à la base du gland.

Elle y puise âprement, en quête
Du nanan qu'elle mourrait pour,
Sive, la crème de quéquette
Caillée aux éclisses d'amour,

Ensuite, après la politesse
Traditionnelle au méat,
Rentre dans la bouche où s'empresse
De la suivre le vit béat,

A crumb or two of shit and cheese
Won't scare away my kind of pluck,
My nose, my mouth, from any crease
Or rut in the fair field of fuck.

I like that cheery puckered flesh,
In fact, my lovers' reeking flues,
That smell like apples, sharp and fresh,
Full of fermenting healthy juice.

There my undaunted tongue goes tense
Over the sweets of long red hairs,
Self-conscious in a lovely sense,
And liquidates its deepest cares,

Then licks the ragged seam, and balls,
With *largo* feelings, broad and slow,
And warps up round the column, stalls
Under the gland, and takes a blow.

Roughly it roots there, mad to find
Clinging around love's cheesy box
The grub to which it's so inclined,
Namely, the clotted cream of cocks.

Then, an old-fashioned compliment
To the red slit we've all come through,
And back in my mouth it goes. Content,
The Blessed Prick pushes in too,

Débordant de foutre, qu'avale
Ce moi, confit en onction,
Parmi l'extase sans rivale
De cette bénédiction!

1891

9   'Il est mauvais coucheur et ce m'est une
     joie...'

Il est mauvais coucheur et ce m'est une joie
De le bien sentir, lorsqu'il est la fière proie
Et le fort commensal du meilleur des sommeils
Sans fausses couches—nul besoin!—et sans réveils,
Si près de moi, comme agressif et soufflant d'aise,
Si près, si près de moi que je crois qu'il me baise,
En quelque sorte, avec son gros vit que je sens
Dans mes cuisses et sur mon ventre frémissants
Si nous nous trouvons face à face, et s'il se tourne
De l'autre côté, tel qu'un bon pain qu'on enfourne
Son cul délicieusement rêveur ou non,
Soudain, mutin, malin, hutin, putain, son nom
De Dieu de cul, d'ailleurs choyé, m'entre en le ventre,
Provocateur et me rend bandeur comme un diantre,
Ou si je lui tourne le mien semble vouloir
M'enculer ou, si dos à dos, son nonchaloir
Brutal et gentil colle à mes fesses ses fesses,
Et mon vit, de bonheur, tu mouilles, puis t'affaisses
Et rebande et remouille,—infini dans cet us.

Heureux moi! *Totus in benigno positus!*

1891

Busily gushing spunk, which I,
Steeped in the holy unction, take,
Enraptured with the ecstasy
Of such a blessing for fuck's sake!

9   'He's an awkward bedfellow and I love
     to keep . . .'

He's an awkward bedfellow and I love to keep
Feeling him there, proud captive of my sleep,
Strong partner in the best of companies
(No small-hour waking, no miscarriages),
So near me, like a threat, contentedly
Growling, so near I think he's kissing me
With his great prick whose little red mouth lies
Wet on my quivering belly or my thighs
If we're confronted; if he's turned himself,
Like a good loaf slid down the oven shelf
His arse (perhaps in some sweet dream of lust)
And doughy cheeks (in fact, well-kneaded) thrust
Suddenly in my lap and with a thump
Pump and provoke a steeple from my stump;
Or if I turn away, he seems . . . he tries . . .
To thread my ring; if back to back, with nice
Animal carelessness he claps his bum
To mine, so (overjoyed) I rise and come
And sink and rise again in endless stands.

Happy? My whole world lies in His kind hands.

Autant certes la femme gagne
A faire l'amour en chemise,
Autant alors cette compagne
Est-elle seulement de mise

A la condition expresse
D'un voile, court, délinéant
Cuisse et mollet, téton et fesse
Et leur truc un peu trop géant,

Ne s'écartant, de sorte nette,
Qu'en faveur du con, seul divin,
Pour le coup et pour la minette,
Et tout le reste en elle, est vain.

A bien considérer les choses,
Ce manque de proportions,
Ces effets trop blancs et trop roses ...
Faudrait que nous en convinssions,

Autant le jeune homme profite
Dans l'intérêt de sa beauté,
Prêtre d'Eros ou néophyte,
D'aimer en toute nudité.

Admirons cette chair splendide,
Comme intelligente, vibrant,
Intrépide et comme timide
Et, par un privilège grand

As women, surely, gain so much
From making love in lingerie,
These comrades of the common touch
Are only in good form, for me,

On strict condition of some veil,
Quite short, that outlines but confounds
Detail of thigh, calf, tit and tail
(Their sandwich of such giant rounds),

And never clearly parts unless
The cunt, their only heavenly use—
The rest of them is meaningless—
Invites a gander, or a goose.

For anyone who cares to think
Of their imbalances and lacks,
Their crude effects of white and pink,
Must yield to the aesthetic facts:

Young men are wiser to invest
(The novice and the one who knows)
Their beauty's simple interest
In making love without their clothes.

Admire this brilliant flesh—that thrill
As if it thinks—so tremulous
And shy, and yet unshakeable;
And, by a grace that's granted us

Sur toute chair, la féminine
Et la bestiale,—vrai beau!—
O cette grâce qui fascine
D'être multiple sous la peau,

Jeu des muscles et du squelette,
Pulpe ferme, souple tissu,
Elle interprète, elle complète
Tout sentiment soudain conçu.

Elle se bande en la colère,
Et raide et molle tour à tour,
Souci de se plaire et de plaire,
Se tend et détend dans l'amour.

Et, quand la mort la frappera,
Cette chair qui me fut un dieu,
Comme auguste, elle fixera
Ses éléments, en marbre bleu!

1891

Above all flesh, both feminine
And animal (because they hide
True beauty deep beneath the skin),
The fascinations of inside:

The play of thews and skeleton,
Firm brawn, and lithe nets where it's caught—
How it completes and comments on
Feelings as soon as they are thought!

It stiffens, angry, at attacks,
And softens when the stress is eased,
Just as in love it can relax
And rise, to please or to be pleased,

And when death strikes it down at last,
This flesh I worshipped at, and knew,
How grand its members are, made fast
In that dull marble veined with blue!

Même quand tu ne bandes pas,
Ta queue encor fait mes délices
Qui pend, blanc d'or, entre tes cuisses,
Sur tes roustons, sombres appas.

—Couilles de mon amant, sœurs fières
A la riche peau de chagrin,
D'un brun et rose et purpurin,
Couilles farceuses et guerrières,

Et dont la gauche balle un peu
Tout petit peu plus bas que l'autre,
D'un air roublard et bon apôtre,
A quelles donc fins, nom de Dieu?—

Elle est dodue ta quéquette,
Et veloutée, du pubis
Au prépuce fermant le pis,
Aux trois quarts, d'une rose crête.

Elle se renfle un brin au bout
Et dessine sous la peau douce
Le gland gros comme un demi-pouce
Montrant ses lèvres juste au bout.

Après que je l'aurai baisée
En tout amour reconnaissant,
Laisse ma main, la caressant,
La saisir d'une prise osée,

Even without presenting arms
Your shrunken cock is my delight:
Between your thighs a golden white,
Draped on your bollocks' swarthy charms.

—Dear lover's balls, proud sisters, dressed
In crumpled shagreen, pinky-brown
With purplish shadows in the down,
Balls full of humour, fizz, and zest,

Though one, the left, is misaligned
And swinging lower makes me think
This scrotum has a knowing wink,
But God knows what it's got in mind!—

It's plump, your little prick, and sleek
As velvet, from the pubic mound
To where the foreskin closes round
The tip, and crowns the rosy peak.

It swells a little at the end
Under the soft skin, sketching out
The gland, an inch long, with a pout
Of red lips showing at the end.

After I've bowed at length and kissed
The rod with loving gratitude,
Let my caressing hand grow rude
And seize it in a daring fist

Pour, soudain, la décalotter;
En sorte que, violet tendre,
Le Gland joyeux, sans plus attendre,
Splendidement vienne éclater;

Et puis elle, en bonne bougresse,
Accélère le mouvement
Et Jean-nu-tête en un moment
De se remettre à la redresse.

Tu bandes! C'est ce que voulaient
Ma bouche et mon cul: choisis, maître.
Une simple douce, peut-être?
C'est ce que mes dix doigts voulaient.

Cependant le vit, mon idole,
Tend, pour le rite et pour le cul—
Te, à mes mains, ma bouche et mon cul
Sa forme adorable d'idole.

1891

And then suddenly doff its cap
So that your tender violet bud
Bursts out, not waiting for more blood,
Joyfully beaming from your lap;

And then (good-natured little sod!)
Speeds up the movement, going hard
Till there! it's back again on guard,
Bareheaded Jack, the risen god.

You're standing now! And that's the wish
Of mouth and arsehole: master, choose.
Or else the plain but sweet abuse
Ten neighbour-loving fingers wish?

Meanwhile to hands and mouth and hole
For prone or supine orisons
The idol that I reverence
Tenders its shapely totem-pole.

12 'Dans ce café bondé d'imbéciles, nous deux...'

Dans ce café bondé d'imbéciles, nous deux,
Seuls, nous représentions le soi-disant hideux
Vice d'être «pour homme» et, sans qu'ils s'en doutassent
Nous encaguions ces cons avec leur air bonasse,
Leurs normales amours et leur morale en toc,
Cependant que, branlés et de taille et d'estoc,
A tire-larigot, à gogo, par principes
Toutefois, voilés par les flocons de nos pipes
(Comme autrefois Héra copulait avec Zeus),
Nos vits, tels que des nez joyeux de Karragheus
Qu'eussent mouchés nos mains d'un geste délectable,
Éternuaient des jets de foutre sous la table.

1891

12   'In that café crowded with fools we stood...'

In that café crowded with fools we stood
(Just us two) for the hideous turpitude
Of liking men: they never thought, the cunts,
We shat on their dim-witted innocence,
Their standard loves, their tinny golden rules.
While holding to our principles and tools
We swung and parried to our hearts' content,
Veiled in a cloud our peaceful pipes had sent—
Like Zeus and Hera in their nebulous bed—
Till our two Punch's noses, glad and red,
Wiped by our fingers with delightful squeezes
Under the table jetted great white sneezes.

13 Dizain ingénu (1860)

O souvenir d'enfance et le lait nourricier
Et ô l'adolescence et son essor princier!
Quand j'étais tout petit garçon, j'avais coutume
Pour évoquer la Femme et bercer l'amertume
De n'avoir qu'une queue imperceptible, bout
Dérisoire, prépuce immense sous quoi bout
Tout le sperme à venir, ô terreur sébacée!
De me branler avec cette bonne pensée
D'une bonne d'enfant à motte de velours.

Depuis je décalotte et me branle toujours!

13   Virgin verses (1860)

O childhood memories—drinking milk at meals!—
And adolescence, high on high ideals!
When still a boy, imagining the scene
A woman offers, and to soothe the spleen
Of having a wet splinter of a cock
Capped with a great big foreskin where my stock
Of seed bubbles, a soapy source of fear—
I used to wank to the Platonic Idea
Of a nanny with a crotch of corduroy.

And ever since . . . caps off, for the same joy!

O mes amants,
   Simples natures,
   Mais quels tempéraments!
Consolez-moi de ces mésaventures.
   Reposez-moi de ces littératures;
Toi, gosse pantinois, branlons-nous en argot,
   Vous, gas des champs, patoisez-moi l'écot,
Des pines au cul et des plumes qu'on taille,
   Livrons-nous dans les bois touffus
         La grande bataille
         Des baisers confus.
Vous, rupins, faisons des langues en artistes
      Et merde aux discours tristes
      Des pédants et des cons.
      (Par cons, j'entends les imbéciles,
      Car les autres cons sont de mise
      Même pour nous, les difficiles,
   Les spéciaux, les servants de la bonne Église
      Dont le pape serait Platon
      Et Socrate un protonotaire.
   Une femme par-ci par-là, c'est le bon ton
   Et les concessions n'ont jamais rien perdu.
      Puis, comme dit l'autre, à chacun son dû,

Oh my lovers,
Simple chaps,
But oh what characters!
Console me for a life's mishaps;
Give me a rest from all those books.
You, Paris kid, let's wank in slang;
You from the fields, in your provincial twang
Tell me the bill for all our foocks,
The cocks up arses and the old quill pen
Trimmed to a point for gentlemen:
And in the woods, the bushy woods, let's join
The battle of the lip and loin,
The tangled scrum
Of kiss and come.
And you, you well-dressed pricks,
Let's swop a few deep licks
Like artists, at the stage door of the bum,
And damn the glum
Remarks of pedants and of cunts.
(By cunts here, I mean bloody fools—
The other cunts are quite in place, in all respects,
Even by us peculiar tools
And choosy servants of the best of sects,
Whose pope is Plato, I suppose,
With Socrates
One of the Secretary-Nuncios.
Having a woman now and then's well-bred,
And giving in you don't give up a thing.
Besides, as someone said,
Give every man his due,

Et les femmes ont, mon Dieu, droit à notre gloire.
Soyons-leur doux
Entre deux coups,
Puis, revenons à notre affaire).
O mes enfants bien-aimés, vengez-moi
Par vos caresses sérieuses
Et vos culs et vos nœuds, régals vraiment de roi,
De toutes ces viandes creuses
Qu'offre la rhétorique aux cervelles breneuses
De ces tristes copains qui ne savent pourquoi.
Ne métaphorons pas, foutons,
Pelotons-nous bien les roustons,
Rinçons nos glands, faisons ripailles
Et de foutre et de merde et de fesses et de cuisses.

And women too,
God knows, have got a right to share
Our glory. So let's use
Them gently, between screws,
And then return to our affair.)
Oh my young darlings, help me get
My own back in your grave caresses,
Among your arses
And tasty tarses,
With the delicious messes
And dainty dishes of a king—
Help me forget
The empty stuffing of those hollow meats
That rhetoric puts out for tender
To those whose brains, fouled up like babies' seats,
Have still not found the best thing on their beats,
Sad sad old pals who still don't know what's what in gender.
But bugger metaphors! let's screw—
It's bollock-time for me and you;
Knock up, a lively stroke or two,
To wet our pricks and start the feast off right;
Tuck in to come and shite
To buttocks and to thighs.

Le sonnet du trou du cul

PAR PAUL VERLAINE ET ARTHUR RIMBAUD

Obscur et froncé comme un œillet violet
Il respire, humblement tapi parmi la mousse,
Humide encor d'amour qui suit la pente douce
Des fesses blanches jusqu'au bord de son ourlet.

Des filaments pareils à des larmes de lait
Ont pleuré, sous l'autan cruel qui les repousse,
A travers de petits caillots de marne rousse,
Pour s'en aller où la pente les appelait.

Ma bouche s'accoupla souvent à sa ventouse,
Mon âme, du coït matériel jalouse,
En fit son larmier fauve et son nid de sanglots.

C'est l'olive pâmée et la flûte câline,
C'est le tube où descend la céleste praline,
Chanaan féminin dans les moîteurs éclos!

Lines on the arsehole: a sonnet

By Paul Verlaine (octet) and Arthur Rimbaud (sextet)

Crumpled like a carnation, mauve and dim
It breathes, cowering humbly in the moss
Still wet with love which trickles down across
The soft slope of white buttocks to its rim.

Threads like long tears of milk blown radiantly
Out by the cruel gust that turns them back
Weep home again along the cambered track
Through reddish clinkers and wild dilberry.

My mouth mates often with this breathing-hole.
While matter goes and comes, my jealous soul
Makes tawny tears there in its nest of sighs:

This olive in a swoon, this flute whose stop
Teases the tube where heaven's soft-centres drop,
This female Promised Land where warm springs rise.

Notes

THE VOCABULARY OF OBSCENITY is not easy (one sympathizes with the German translator who thought 'roustons' meant 'tits'), so the reader may be glad to know some of my reference books: Alfred Delvau's *Dictionnaire érotique moderne* (nouvelle éd., 1891; Slatkine Reprints, 1968); Francis Grose's *A Classical Dictionary of the Vulgar Tongue* (1785; but the 1811 edition has been reprinted by Follett Publishing Co., Chicago, 1971); and Eric Partridge's *Dictionary of Slang and Unconventional English* (4th ed., Routledge & Kegan Paul, 1951). John S. Farmer and W. E. Henley's *Slang and its Analogues* . . . (7 vols., 1890–1904) was more amusement than help (why would the French call the arse a schelingophone?), but it provided the odd explanation, as did Alex Comfort's *The Joy of Sex* (Quartet Books, 1975).

For convenience, page-references are occasionally given to the Pléiade edition of Verlaine's *Œuvres poétiques complètes*, texte établi et annoté par Y.-G. Le Dantec, édition révisée, complétée et présentée par Jacques Borel (Gallimard, 1962). The *Club du meilleur livre* text is referred to as CML. I have also been much aided by Jacques Robichez's magisterial annotated edition (Garnier, 1969) of Verlaine's eight main books of poetry, and by the notes of 'Jissey' to his own critical edition of the *Œuvres libres*, published *sous le manteau* at Metz in 1949.

Femmes

OUVERTURE (page 18)

Stanza 5, line 3: The word 'hure' (boar's head) was used of Verlaine's appearance in 1886: in *Le Petit Bottin des Lettres et des Arts* edited by Félix Fénéon and Laurent Tailhade (quoted in George Zayed's edition of Verlaine's *Lettres inédites à Charles Morice*, 2nd ed., 1969, p. 11).

A CELLE QUE L'ON DIT FROIDE (page 22)

Pléiade, p. 532.
I have preferred the manuscript's readings in two places. The CML readings are:
Stanza 4, line 4: ends with full stop.
Stanza 12, line 1: Quant au Point—froide, ô non pas fraîche,

It has been suggested that the poem is 'about' Verlaine's wife Mathilde Mauté, who was indeed a schoolgirl, aged seventeen, when he married her on 11 August 1870. However, other poems considered to be 'about' Mathilde and also written after their divorce in 1885 and her remarriage in 1886 are so different in tone that the identification seems unlikely. (See 'Le sonnet de l'homme au sable' and 'A Madame ***', both in *Parallèlement*—Pléiade, pp. 495 and 515.)

Stanza 4, line 4: The comma at the end is surely right because the following five stanzas are part of this sentence, linked to 'à travers' by a series of 'jusqu'à' phrases. Verlaine loved a long sentence. Moreover, it would be uncharacteristically clumsy versification to have 'beau' agreeing with 'odeur': 'beau' must be looking forward (still clumsy, but much less) to 'Chose'.

The word 'éclisse' deserves a note. Deep down, the word means a bit of wood (e.g. in the middle ages, fragments of a shattered lance), but came to mean objects made of split-wood like baskets, small presses for making cream cheese, and 'pots' for catching lobsters, etc. Creel can be used in this sense, though I would have preferred a word of wider meaning, as the idea of cheese (and bodily matter) is probably present as well as salty wickerwork.

Stanza 11, line 1: 'nœud' (knot) is both a cliché of love poetry and a vulgarism referring to the male genitals. 'Incoercible' (incompressible) is hard to render, therefore.

PARTIE CARRÉE (page 26)

Stanza 4, line 3: 'Vainqueurs'. From the frequency with which the word 'vaincre' and its derivatives occur in these poems (and elsewhere in Verlaine—e.g. as 'le piston vainqueur' in 'Chevaux de bois', in *Romances sans paroles*—Pléiade p. 200; or as 'Je suis ton vaincu' in 'Auburn'—*Parallèlement*, 'Filles' IV—Pléiade p. 494), one would think there must be some specific sexual meaning of the word. But there is none that I can discover (apart from the cliché about conquest), and possibly one merely notices more Verlaine's liking for 'vaincre' and the pun of 'vain cu' as a result of the (presumably deliberate) exclusion of words of the 'aimer' family (which are rare in this book).

TRIOLETS À UNE VERTU . . . (page 28)

Lines 1–2 of stanza 3 are a quotation from La Fontaine (*Fables*, V, 3, lines 1–2), or rather from an 1890 school edition which caused a scandal by substituting 'L'on' for 'Dieu'.

The two Latin words in the last stanza mean 'the fields enough', i.e. 'the fields have had enough to drink' (*sat prata biberunt*), and come from the last line of Virgil's third *Eclogue*. Verlaine quoted the line also in *Invectives* XXVIII, 'Thomas Diafoirus' (Pléiade, p. 927), and translated it in 'Vieux Coppées' III, line 1 (Pléiade, p. 298).

GOÛTS ROYAUX (page 32)

Pléiade, p. 534.
CML reads 'Des pieds roux . . .' in line 20; but other printed texts I have seen read 'doux'. The CML editors don't refer to the manuscript to support their word, and I think 'doux' is much better; so I was delighted to be informed by Professor Zayed that 'roux' is a misprint dating back to the first edition of the Pléiade Verlaine by Y.-G. Le Dantec in 1938.

133

FILLES I (page 34)

Pléiade, p. 535.
Composed 22 October 1889, originally intended as part of the group 'Filles' in a new edition of *Parallèlement* (according to the manuscript).

Lines 39–40: 'à potron-minet' means 'very early in the morning' (etymologically, 'as soon as the cat shows its arse'); Verlaine has modified the phrase so as to bring in 'faire la minette' (which means 'gamahucher'—using your tongue like a cat).

FILLES II (page 38)

Stanza 8: The crafty/simple oxymoron occurs also in the second poem of *Hombres* ('Mille e tre', stanza 3). Line 2 seems to mean 'you can *make* your eyes water but they water by themselves too'—but this is complicated by the fact that an obscene meaning of 'mouiller' (to come, have an orgasm) is present as well.

A MADAME *** (page 44)

This title was used by Verlaine four times; on the other three occasions (Pléiade, pp. 165, 495, 984) he had his wife Mathilde in mind. There is also a Madame *** in Rimbaud's *Les Illuminations*, with a piano ('Après le déluge') and with Verlainean schoolgirls ('Dévotion').

Stanza 5, line 2: The French noun 'pis' can only be translated 'teat' or 'dug', but the associated image seems to be of something flesh-coloured and finger-like, a cow's teat, not the flat human medallion. The whole stanza conveys then a picture of a broad hairy muzzle butting and sucking at an udder. 'Pis' appears without more ado as equivalent to 'vit' (penis) in poem 11 of *Hombres*.

Stanza 6: A 'boule de gomme' is a throat-sweet or cough-lozenge (Robert's dictionary). Verlaine perhaps invented this use of the phrase (see also 'Régals'), which is not in Delvau or elsewhere.

134

Vas Unguentatum (page 46)

The title is not a phrase from St Jerome's Latin version of the Bible, but most of the associations conglomerated in it are Biblical: the weaker vessel (to which other vessels defer), blood-vessels, altar vessels ('autel' can mean 'la nature de la femme' according to Delvau), the Lord's anointed, with unguents fit for kings or those who are not amused.

Idylle High-Life (page 50)

Line 1: 'galopin(e)' appears here to have no class connotation, though it does in 'Poème saturnien' in *Parallèlement* (Pléiade, p. 509).

Stanza 7, line 2: 'Oaristys' is a Greek word meaning friendly conversation, with sexual overtones, and was already used in Verlaine's first book, in the poem 'Vœu' (Pléiade, p. 62). He might have come across it as the title of a charming poem of seduction by Theocritus (*Idyll* 27) or in André Chénier's translation (*Bucoliques* XV). (The poem was also translated by Dryden, marvellously—see J. Kinsley's edition of *The Poems of John Dryden*, 1958, vol. 1, p. 427.)

Billet à Lily (page 56)

Pléiade, p. 537.
First published in *La Plume*, 1 September 1890. 'Lily' was probably Caroline Teisen, from Verlaine's birthplace Metz, which explains the first line.

Pour Rita (page 58)

Rita is presumably the same 'fleur du Brésil' who decorated Verlaine's hat 'd'un ruban moiré, moins pourtant que ses sombres cheveux' shortly before his trip to Aix-les-Bains in 1889, so amusingly described in his *Chroniques de l'hôpital*, 5 (Pléiade *prose*, p. 261).

Stanza 7, line 1: 'féminines' (CML) is a misprint.

Stanza 7, line 4: 'en défaut' is used of hounds losing the scent; 'jamais en défaut', as well as meaning 'never off the scent', implies an obsession with the scent; and over all this hangs lightly the secret bisexual joke that if he's attracted to a person, he can't lose, if they respond, whichever sex they turn out to be. Irony apart, the idea has a certain humane grandeur; but not in this poem.

RÉGALS (page 70)

Line 25: CML text reads 'Tant que de la gueule que du blaire', which is evidently hypermetric. Other printed texts lack the first 'que'.

GAMINERIES (page 74)

Note on versification: As Verlaine used only feminine rhymes in the homosexual sonnet sequence 'Les amies' (reprinted in *Parallèlement*) and only masculine rhymes in other homosexual poems like 'Balanide I' (*Hombres*) and 'L'impudent' (*Parallèlement*), so perhaps here he strengthens the bisexual tone of the title and first stanza by using all feminine or all masculine rhymes in alternate *stanzas*, instead of alternating the rhymes line by line as is the classical usage. (He does the same thing with the rhymes in the poem about Rimbaud, 'Laeti et errabundi', also in *Parallèlement*—Pléiade, p. 522.)

Stanza 1, line 1: The word 'commode' is the only reference in these poems to health. Verlaine used the word similarly in a letter to Charles Morice of 30 October 1886 (George Zayed's edition, p. 85): 'Avec ma jambe malade ce n'est guère commode fructueusement "turbiner." (Courses aux journaux, théâtre, etc., que j'y aille donc!!)'

Stanza 1, line 3: 'Riding St George. The woman uppermost in the amorous congress, that is, the dragon upon St George. This is said to be the way to get a bishop.' (Francis Grose)

Stanza 10, line 2: Verlaine seems to be deriving 'faire postillon' from the mediaeval Latin word 'postilla', a gloss on the gospel, rather than from 'postilions'. Delvau is no help on this point (not being interested in etymology).

HOMMAGE DÛ (page 78)

Line 12 was cannibalized to form line 28 of *Odes en son honneur* X (Pléiade, p. 772).
Line 16: 'bouffé' here seems to mean engorged or swollen, rather than guzzled or gorged on.

MORALE EN RACCOURCI (page 80)

Line 2: '. . . de beau tétons bandants' (CML) is a misprint, caused perhaps by the compositor's noticing the imperfect rhyme and the awkwardly inconsistent rhyme-scheme.

Hombres

Everyone from Antoine Adam to Georges Zayed seems sure there is no puzzle in this title: it is simply the Spanish for *Hommes*.

'O ne blasphème pas . . .' (poem 1, page 84)

Verlaine's manuscript (followed without comment by CML) does not close the inverted commas opened for History's speech (*stanza 6, line 2*). The best place to close them might be after line 2 of the last stanza (where we surely have Verlaine's voice in the reference back to line 1), or, more likely, at the end of stanza 6 itself, since the special pleading in stanza 7 and the phrase 'notre ère' in stanza 8 seem rather too personal for the voice of History.

Stanza 7: Verlaine could have picked up the loopy idea that Shakespeare was homosexual (like Bacon!) from several nineteenth-century sources, but he was already talking about Shakespeare's 'troubling sonnets' in his preface to Henri d'Argis' novel *Sodome* (1888), so he didn't get the idea from Oscar Wilde's story 'The Portrait of Mr W.H.' (published in outline in *Blackwood's*, July 1889). The mistake about the date of the sonnets (they were written long before *Hamlet, Lear* and *Othello*) is presumably a deduction from their publication date (after *Hamlet* and *Lear*, but still before *Othello*).

Stanza 8: I have not followed Verlaine's departure from the rhyme-scheme, which is incidentally the same as that of a more successful poem on the same lines, 'Ces passions' in *Parallèlement* (Pléiade, p. 521).

Wagner is mentioned as an aid to the identification of Ludwig II of Bavaria (his patron), on whose death in 1886 Verlaine had been commissioned to write a sonnet for the *Revue wagnérienne*. (It was reprinted in his book *Amour* next to the more famous sonnet 'Parsifal'—Pléiade, pp. 426–7.)

MILLE E TRE (page 88)

This title is a phrase from Da Ponte's libretto for *Don Giovanni*. It occurs in the famous catalogue aria, in which Don Juan's servant Leporello lists his master's sexual victories in various countries. Verlaine alluded to the phrase again in a prose piece about an amorous dog in *Mémoires d'un veuf* ('Chiens').

Stanza 4: The repetition of the rhyme-word 'joyeuses' is intentional. There are several such repetitions in this book, all merely annoying and seemingly lazy, in my view, but there is one in *Sagesse* (III, vi) where the affectation combines beautifully with simple regret.

Stanza 6: I apologize to my American readers for the pun on 'routes' (pronounced 'roots' east of the Atlantic), and to all my readers for my squeamishness in not confronting 'more divine than infernal, more infernal than divine' more directly.

Stanza 8, line 4: The manuscript reads 'non pareils' (which may or may not include the two senses I unfold in the translation). The CML editors follow the first edition (which seems to have no authority), reading 'sans pareils', thus deleting an awkward double meaning (or joke).

Stanza 12, line 1: 'Se faire' is an idiom which really means to 'become' or 'get'. Verlaine plays on the literal meaning, and I have followed.

BALANIDE I (page 92)

The title is not of course a reference to the *Balanidae* (acorn-shells) but to the word on which the whole poem is a riddle: 'gland' (the French word for acorn, but used popularly to refer to the glans penis).

Line 1 is based on Champsaur's definition of the arsehole: 'C'est le con plus petit', which Verlaine incidentally had scribbled on the back of the front cover of the Fonds Doucet manuscript of *Hombres*.

Stanza 3: 'yssir' (or 'issir', or 'eissir') is replaced in modern French by 'sortir', and only survives in the participle 'issu'. Littré and Robert ignore the word though it is not uncommon in Rabelais. Huguet's examples in *his* dictionary indicate a military emphasis (like the English word 'sortie') with a mediaeval flavour, a feel of knights emerging from castles for a bout.

Stanza 4: 'chœur/cœur' and 'autel/hôtel' are pairs of homonyms. 'Nave/knave' is the nearest corresponding pun in English. 'Cœur' and 'autel' are both in Delvau's dictionary defined as 'la nature de la femme'.

BALANIDE II (page 94)

The numbering of this and subsequent poems (from 4 to 14) is that of the CML editors; I have copied it, though it seems to derive from Léon Vanier's transcript of Verlaine's manuscript. By putting the date after 'Balanide II', Verlaine seems to have wished to indicate that the two poems should be considered a unit, like the two 'Filles' poems. The CML critical apparatus shows also that Verlaine considered calling the second poem 'Balanides'.

Stanza 1: The manuscript and CML have a comma after line 4 instead of line 5: evidently an oversight. Verlaine's occasional use of direct address ('tu') to parts of the body (here his 'cul'; in 'A celle que l'on dit froide', stanzas 4–5, the girl's 'Chose') can be difficult for the modern reader. The manœuvre is very common in Latin verse, for reasons of metre, so it has a classical ring to it, but it can also help produce a rhyme. (See 'Prologue supprimé à un livre d'Invectives', line 4, in *Parallèlement*, 2nd ed., Pléiade, p. 513, or lines 16–19 of *Hombres* poem 9, where this use of the vocative does help him to a rhyme, but then lands him in a syntactical mess.)

Last stanza, line 1: 'Dictame' ('dittany', a plant supposedly full of medicinal virtues) occurs also in Rimbaud's prose piece *Un coeur sous un soutane*, composed in 1870.

Last stanza, line 5 : The translation here attempts to recall the mediaeval meaning of homage as a ceremony affirming that one is the man of one's feudal master. The name of the ceremony, 'hommage de bouche et des mains', lies nicely behind other parts of the poem, too. The undertone seems a likely one for a poet of Verlaine's care with etymologies, but I can also cite his contemporary use of the word 'inféodation' (in the last sentence of 'Souvenirs sur Théodore de Banville', published July 1891). It must be admitted that homage is also paid to a *woman* in *Parallèlement* ('Filles IV, Auburn'—Pléiade, p. 493); but then, notions of submission and fidelity are very widespread in Verlaine.

SUR UNE STATUE (page 98)

Pléiade, p. 512.
Stanza 3, line 2 : Revard is a mountain near Aix-les-Bains, but presumably Verlaine only mentions it because it sounds dreamy.

Stanza 3, line 3 : 'Faire la nique' means cocking a snook, but in English an *eye* cannot make this gesture (though it is also called 'taking a sight'), or I can't, even if Verlaine can; though it would make a handy rhyme.

RENDEZVOUS (page 100)

Pléiade, p. 537; an earlier version, dated 1887 and only five stanzas long, is also printed there, p. 1223.

'Monte sur moi . . .' (poem 7, page 104)

Stanza 5, line 3 : 'lourdois', an adjective from Rabelais, meaning rustic or clumsy, and here part of a web of contrasts between sweet weight and heavy-weight and the etymologies of the words.

Stanza 7, line 4 : 'déferle'—in French, waves unfurl, that is, curl-and-break in one verb. (Cf. *Sagesse* III, xiii—Pléiade, p. 284.)

Stanza 8, line 1 : 'Le mien de flux' is an emphatic, colloquial way of saying 'Mon flux'. Two other examples from Verlaine:

Et du meilleur bon sens, celui qu' à la male heure
Sollicite le mien de bon sens de poète!

('Dans les limbes' XII, lines 7–8, Pléiade, p. 838)
and lines 55–6 of 'Prologue supprimé . . .' (*Parallèlement*, 2nd ed.—
Pléiade, p. 514). The dictionaries of Robert and Littré seem not to
mention this use of 'de', but quotations from Daudet, Courteline,
Céline, Giono and Sartre are given by Maurice Grevisse (*Le bon usage*,
9e éd., 1969, p. 936) and P. Dupré (*Encyclopédie du bon français dans
l'usage contemporain*; Paris, Editions de Trévise 1972, p. 595).

'*Il est mauvais coucheur . . .*' (poem 9, page 110)

The first phrase of the poem means 'he's an ugly customer', except that
ugly and customer are both inappropriate.

Last line: Totus in benigno positus. The epigraph of the poem
'Réversibilités' (*Parallèlement*—Pléiade, p. 500) is *Totus in maligno
positus*, and that is a quotation from the Vulgate translation of the First
Epistle of St John, V, 19: 'Scimus quoniam ex Deo sumus: et mundus
totus in maligno positus est.' I translate this: 'We know we are from
God, and the whole world has been put in the power, or the hands, of
the malevolent one—the Devil'; the Authorized Version is even closer
to Verlaine's interpretation: 'And we know that we are of God, and the
whole world lieth in wickedness.' In this poem, by changing a word, and
representing himself as lying in the arms not of the Enemy but of the
Friend of humanity, Verlaine has produced a characteristically
ambiguous blasphemy.

'*Dans ce café . . .*' (poem 12, page 120)

Line 4: 'encaguions' appears as 'incaguions' in 'Chansons pour elle' XVI
(Pléiade, p. 721); again, 'encague' appears in 'Chanson pour elles',
stanza 3 (Pléiade, p. 884). Dictionaries prefer the spelling 'incaguer'.

Line 10: Punch is a poor substitute for Karagöz, the hero of the Turkish shadow theatre. Karagöz plays had been described by Gérard de Nerval in his *Voyage en orient*, 1851 (Les nuits du Ramazan, II—Théâtres et Fêtes, III—Caragueuz; see the Pléiade Nerval, T.2, p. 480) and by Théophile Gautier in his *Constantinople* (chapter XIV—Karagheuz). Verlaine is perhaps spelling from memory.

DIZAIN INGÉNU (page 122)

A 'dizain' is not in fact five couplets, like this poem, but a stanza-form using only four rhymes.

Lines 3–10 date from 1871 or 1872: under the title 'Remembrances' they were entered by Verlaine in the *Album Zutique*, a sort of visitors' book kept by a group of literary friends who called themselves les Zutistes. (See the letter to François Coppée of 18 April 1869, in Verlaine's *Lettres inédites à divers correspondants*, publiées et annotées par Georges Zayed, Genève, Droz, 1976, p. 50. The *Album Zutique* was edited by Pascal Pia and published in Paris by Pauvert in 1962.)

Line 3: 'Quant' (CML) is a misprint.

'O mes amants . . .' (poem 14, page 124)

Line 20: CML has the misprint 'protonoraire'. This La Fontainean pastiche is unfinished: several rhymes are not matched up, and the last line is unmetrical. My interpretation of the phrase 'en artistes' is derived from Delvau's recording that 'entrée des artistes' can mean 'le cul'.

LE SONNET DU TROU DU CUL (page 128)

There is another version of this in the Pléiade Rimbaud (p. 207), as the third of a set of three sonnets called 'Les stupra'. The poem is another *Album Zutique* item, where it described itself as a 'parodie' of a series of sonnets, on the beauties of a lady, by Albert Mérat in his book *L'Idole*.

Line 8: 'clinkers' dates from *c.* 1830 and is still in use, with the same meaning as 'dilberries', which is thus defined by Francis Grose: 'small pieces of excrement adhering to the hairs near the fundament'.

Line 12: 'pâmée' is puzzling until one realizes that 'se pâmer' means 'to pass out while coming' (Delvau) or more specifically 'se branler', as in the last line of 'La Princesse Bérénice' (*Jadis et Naguère*—Pléiade, p. 370).

Line 14: Our reading 'éclos' seems preferable to the Pléiade Rimbaud's 'enclos' if only because it adds another tie with Baudelaire's sonnet *L'idéal*:

Rêve d'Eschyle éclos au climat des autans;
Ou bien toi, grande Nuit, fille de Michel-Ange,
Qui tords paisiblement dans une pose étrange
Tes appas façonnés aux bouches des Titans.

Appendix

THE TWO POEMS added here were first published in 1964, by Georges Zayed, in his edition of Verlaine's *Lettres inédites à Charles Morice*. Because the poems were appended to that book at the last stage of proofing, it was impossible to correct a number of misprints; Professor Zayed has kindly supplied me with correct readings.

The poems had been found by Professor Zayed in the manuscript belonging to Jean Gimpel referred to as the '*Dossier Gimpel*, manuscrit d'*Auculnes*'—this was a title Verlaine had in mind for the book that was finally called *Femmes*. The poem 'Sadisme' was meant for *Femmes*, but was not finished: beneath the last word of it Verlaine had written '3 à faire'; presumably this meant three stanzas. The other poem (which begins with the same line as poem 1 of *Hombres*) had the words 'Parallt nlle édn' written at the top, but it did not of course appear in the new edition of *Parallèlement* (1894), any more than some of the *Femmes* poems which in 1889 Verlaine had thought suitable for that new edition.

'Chant alterné' in the last stanza of the last poem recalls the Virgilian dialogue-poem that Verlaine was thinking about on his Aix-les-Bains trip: 'Idée aussi pour 2d édition de *Parallèlement*. Un dialogue entre éphèbes et vierges, à la Virgile; le cadre me permettra les dernières hardiesses. Intitulé *Chant alterné*' (letter to Cazals, 31 August 1889, Zayed's edition p. 194). As far as is known, this poem was never written, presumably because it seemed better to cover that sort of argumentative and 'bold' ground not in a single complex debate-poem, but in several separate poems, not necessarily polemical—like those that make up *Femmes* and *Hombres*.

By the way, the poem 'Sadisme' ends in mid-stanza (with the word 'ventouses'), but I have ventured to guess the remaining trajectory of the poem and supply an English version. The last six lines on page 149 have no authority, therefore.

I Sadisme

Vous êtes une raffinée
Et je ne suis pas un novice.
Or, voulez-vous? faisons du vice
Par cette nuit vraiment damnée.

Je suis peu sadique entre nous.
Et vous? Point? Bah, soyons l'un brin.
Mais d'abord quelques tours de rein.
Là . . . c'est classique mais c'est doux.

Maintenant, aux tâches augustes!
Dépouillons la nature humaine.
Devenons des bêtes de haine,
Toutes rage, membres et bustes.

Ces caresses fades un peu
Que nous aimâmes, succions,
Lèchements, si nous les foncions?
Fi d'un tête-bêche vieux jeu.

Moi vampire quand toi lamie,
Mords et pompe tant que je pleure,
Moi je pompe et mords tant que meure,
S'il faut, ce toi, mon ennemie.

Sur la peau mordons jusqu'au sang,
Le sang a soif, il est salé,
Pour boire encore plus salé
Mordons et pompons jusqu'au sang.

Sadism

You're a cultivated girl; and I
Didn't start ploughing yesterday.
A hellish night; what do you say
To something vicious? Shall we try?

I'm no great sadist, *entre nous*.
And you? No? Hell, let's chance a bit.
But first some straight bangs, tit to tit,
There . . . very trad, but sweet to do.

Now the solemnities begin:
Strip off all our humanity!
Turn into beasts of hate, so we
Become just maddened limbs, trunks, skin.

Those strokes we long loved well enough,
Lapping and licking, start to pall:
Can't we push on from there at all?
Damn that old-fashioned *soixante-neuf*!

With me a vampire, you a witch,
Bite and suck at me till I cry;
I'll suck and bite you till you die,
If need be, my opponent: bitch!

Bite through the skin to reach the blood:
The blood is thirsty, and tastes salt;
To get a drink with still more salt,
Bite deep and suck right through to blood.

Mais les muqueuses, les muqueuses!
Suçons-les en âpres ventouses

And how the membranes jerk and ooze!
Suck harshly at them like a leech
Until we drop off bloated, each
Drunk on the ichor we transfuse.

But if our eyes meet then we'll join
Like old friends, with a kiss and goose,
While my prick filling with your juice
Remounts your strange, familiar groin.

O ne blasphème pas, poète, et souviens-toi!
Aime la femme, elle est aimable, mais prudence!
Car le jeune homme nu, soit qu'il lutte ou qu'il danse,
Dans l'un et l'autre amour, vu travaillant ou coi,

Gagnera toujours mieux le suffrage des sages
Que quelque fille que ce soit, célèbre pour
Son cul d'ailleurs impropre à la fin de l'amour,
Bon tout au plus à de subalternes usages.

Toute mesure en l'embonpoint, svelte, élégant,
Le cul de tes amants, seule âme de ta vie,
T'emporte mieux que ta chimère poursuivie,
Croupe adorée, au paradis extravagant,

Paradoxale joie, intense et surhumaine,
Sans compter l'offensive enjoyée à ton tour
Et ces régals, tels des gâteaux tout chauds du four,
Dont ta femme ne peut donner que l'ombre vaine.

Dès lors, poète jadis fier pour n'être pas
Le pire des ingrats romps un triste silence,
Chante un chant alterné dont penche la balance
Du côté masculin, toujours un peu plus bas.

Now poet, don't forget: no blasphemies!
Love women, yes, they're lovable all right;
But young men, naked—fit to dance or fight,
Or bare for love each way, for work, for ease—

Will always win the wise aesthetic poll
Over whatever girl, whose famous crotch
Is no fit place for love to stand his watch,
Good at the best for a much baser rôle.

But with its slender chic, so chastely plump,
The male arse can inspire and carry you,
Better than that vain monster you pursue,
Off to queer heavens on its worshipped rump,

To joy that shocks, gripping and more than human,
Not counting the return-attacks of love
And those warm treats like sweetmeats from the stove,
Where empty shadow's offered by a woman.

Come, poet, once so proud: don't let this go
Unthanked; break the sad silence that prevails;
Sing the antiphonal; redress the scales
Where men have always hung a little low.